Mabel Geraldine Woodruffe Peacock

An Index of the Names of the Royalists

Whose Estates were Confiscated During the Commonwealth

Mabel Geraldine Woodruffe Peacock

An Index of the Names of the Royalists
Whose Estates were Confiscated During the Commonwealth

ISBN/EAN: 9783337185978

Printed in Europe, USA, Canada, Australia, Japan

Cover: Foto ©ninafisch / pixelio.de

More available books at **www.hansebooks.com**

INDEX OF ROYALISTS.

INDEX SOCIETY.
PUBLICATIONS, 1878.
II.

AN INDEX

OF THE NAMES OF THE

ROYALISTS WHOSE ESTATES

WERE CONFISCATED DURING THE COMMONWEALTH.

With a Reprint of the Three Confiscation Acts of 1651 and 1652, from Scobell's "Collection of Acts and Ordinances of General Use, from 3rd of November, 1640, to 17th of September, 1656."

compiled by
MABEL G. W. PEACOCK.

LONDON:
PUBLISHED FOR THE INDEX SOCIETY
BY LONGMANS, GREEN & Co., 39, PATERNOSTER ROW.
MDCCCLXXIX.

HERTFORD:
PRINTED BY STEPHEN AUSTIN AND SONS.

PREFACE.

THE various ordinances of the Long Parliament after its rupture with the King were all, or nearly all, of them printed as separate pamphlets or broadsides.

The more important of these before the 13th March, 1643, were collected and printed in a 4to. volume of 954 pages entitled "An Exact Collection of all Remonstrances, Declarations, Votes, Orders, Ordinances, Proclamations, Petitions, Messages, Answers, and other Remarkable Passages between the King's most Excellent Majesty, and his High Court of Parliament. . . . . . London, Printed for Edward Husbands, T. Warren, R. Best, and are to be sold at the Middle Temple, Grays Inne Gate, and the White Horse in Pauls Churchyard, 1643."

This was followed by a folio volume of 943 pages and 24 pages of appendix, entitled "A Collection of all the publicke Orders, Ordinances and Declarations of both Houses of Parliament, from the Ninth of March 1642 untill December 1646. Together with severall of His Majesties Proclamations and other Papers Printed at Oxford . . . . . . London. Printed by T. W. for Ed: Husband, Printer to the Honorable House of Commons, And are to be sold at his shop at the signe of the Golden Dragon in Fleetstreet Nere the Temple Gate 1646."

Several smaller collections of similar documents were published during the time covered by these two volumes. In the last year of the reign of the Protector Oliver, they were all superseded, for the practical business purposes of the time, by the appearance of " A Collection of Acts and Ordinances of General Use, made in the Parliament begun and held at Westminster the third day of November, Anno 1640 and since, unto the Adjournment of the Parliament begun and holden the 17th of September, Anno 1656. . . . . . By Henry Scobell Esq; Clerk of the Parliament. Examined by the Original Records, And now printed by Special Order of Parliament. London, Printed by Henry Hills and John Field, Printers to His Highness the Lord Protector. 1658." The three collections contain a vast amount of information bearing on the history of the disturbed time to which they relate, but their indexes are almost useless, and consequently they have been of but little service to historians. It is much to be wished that a complete collection of the Ordinances and Acts of Parliament issued between the beginning of the Civil War and the Restoration should be printed for the use of historical students. Though no part of the Statutes of the realm, these treasonable papers have far more living interest than the Acts of many Parliaments whose doings have been strictly legal. If, however, there be no hope of our ever possessing so useful a compilation, it would be well if an index were given of the three volumes above mentioned, in one alphabet.

The Confiscation Acts here reprinted are taken from the

work of Scobell, and have been copied entire, except that the notes in the margins of the pages, which contain no information beyond what is given in the text, have been left out as useless.

The proceedings against the Royalists during the Civil War, the Commonwealth, and the Protectorate, are very voluminous and intricate. Until the details of those days are more carefully arranged than at present, it will be impossible to give a full and clear account of what took place.

The first proceedings against the supporters of the King's party noticed in the Journals of the House of Commons seems to be the Ordinance of the 15th March, 1643, for sequestering the estates of papists, bishops, delinquents, and notorious malignants. The notices in the Index to the Journals of the House of Commons of proceedings against delinquents occupy more than six closely printed folio pages.

At first the Royalists were admitted to compound for their estates—that is, they were heavily fined, in what seemed to the men in power a just proportion to their political offences, but as time went on, and feelings became more bitter and passions more fierce, the fines were made heavier. It is probable that the extreme measure of confiscation was not carried out against any (except very prominent people) who had been engaged in the war before the surrender of the King to the Scotch, but who had afterwards abstained from any demonstration against the ruling powers and held aloof from actively sharing in the troubles that followed. It is evident that these persons were regarded in a different light from those men who afterwards took part in the insurrections in Kent and Essex, the men who were concerned in the Pontefract Castle adventure and the raid into the Isle of Axholme, or those who fought at Preston and Worcester. These latter were looked on as rebels, and it was felt that their struggle for the purpose of overturning the government had been so highly dangerous, in spite of its failure, that it was needful for the welfare of the State that they should not for the future find means of mischief ready to their hands. It is scarcely possible to say how far the authorities were guided by the motive of preserving the Commonwealth from constant warfare within herself, and how far they were moved by the desire of obtaining money for the Navy, payment of the long-standing arrears of the Army, and other State expenses, without incurring the odium of still heavier taxation. The latter motive has been attributed to them not only by the Royalist writers, but by others whose feelings have been strongly on the winning side.

I believe these severe Confiscation Acts were passed mainly as a protection against civil war, but certainly they must also be regarded as measures by which the urgent need for money was to be satisfied without taxing too oppressively those who were loyal to the government of the Parliament. We have not now before us, and possibly may never have, sufficient means for judging in what degree each of these two motives influenced the men in power. Probably they scarcely knew themselves; some may have looked merely for the complete suppression of revolt, others may have seen that this was impossible unless their own friends were relieved from the heavy burdens that necessity would lay on them, if other means were not found for paying the public debts.

A few words must be said as to the form in which many of the names appear. At first it had been intended to put what is commonly held to be the correct spelling of the names in the text, within square brackets, and in one or two cases this has been done, but to carry out this plan would be impossible without an amount of labour and consequent delay which would be out of all proportion to the good to be gained. The spelling of surnames, and sometimes of the names of places, was very irregular, it is still arbitrary in a high degree, and families come of the same stock at the present time often spell their names after a different fashion. To have undertaken to ascertain the manner in which the clerks who draughted these Acts should have spelt the names of the Parliament's victims would not only have entailed almost endless research among records and county and family histories, but would also have required the settlement of the question how the possessors of these names should have spelt them, for so little was uniformity of spelling regarded in former times that it is no uncommon thing to find one man signing his name in three or four forms. This habit—it can hardly have been the result of carelessness alone—was of an earlier date, and continued some time after the Civil War. In the will of my own collateral ancestor, John Peacock, of Epworth, in the Isle of Axholme, which was executed in 1542, his surname is spelt six different ways; and Denis Grenville, Dean of Durham from 1684 to 1691, much of whose correspondence has been published by the Surtees Society, spelt his surname in four various fashions, and it occurs in a fifth form in Le Neve's *Fasti Ecclesiæ Anglicanæ* (ed. 1854, vol. iii. p. 300). It will also have been observed that the publisher of the two volumes of Parliamentarian Ordinances calls himself Husbands on the title of the first volume and Husband on that of the second. Men may have thought it looked picturesque to vary the letters of their names, but in the case of place-names the differences must frequently be attributed to the ignorance of the writer, for they are often further from the true sound of the word than would be possible if it had been familiar to the ear.

It may be of use to some persons to know that the Royalist Composition papers in Her Majesty's Public Record Office contain accounts as to the real estates of a great number, probably of all the persons whose names occur in the following lists.

These Royalist Composition papers consist of a large series of documents relating to the fines levied on estates, and the confiscations during the Civil War period and the Commonwealth. They often contain minute particulars as to the lands and estates of the sufferers, which are of incalculable value to persons engaged in the study of local history and genealogy. There is a most excellent Manuscript Index to them preserved in the Literary Search Room. I believe that an analysis of the whole of these papers will be published in forthcoming volumes of the Calendars of Domestic State Papers.[1]

In 1655 Thomas Dring, a London bookseller, published "at the signe of the George in Fleet-street near Cliffords Inne"— "A Catalogue of the Lords, Knights and Gentlemen who have compounded for their estates." There is reason for believing

---

[1] The advisability of printing an Index to these Composition Papers was urged upon the Committee of the Index Society, but before undertaking the work they made inquiries at the Record Office, when it was found that a full description of these Papers was to be included in the series of Calendars. All interested in these valuable documents may therefore expect to obtain a Calendar from the able and experienced hands of Mrs. Everett Green, with an Index of a more accurate and comprehensive character than the Manuscript one now in use.—H. B. W.

that this is very imperfect even as a mere name list. It is, moreover, one of the most inaccurately printed books in the English language. It is probably an impression of a very rough list, prepared by some Government clerk of the period, which had strayed from proper custody. It seems hardly possible that the strange blunders it contains can all be mere printers' errors. They may be best accounted for on the supposition that the original **'copy'** had never been prepared for the press, and **that** the manuscript was so carelessly written that the printer could not read many portions of it. This almost worthless book was reprinted at Chester in 1733, and this edition is said to contain some names not found in the earlier one.

Mabel Geraldine Woodruffe Peacock.

Bottesford Manor, Brigg,
    October, 1878.

ROYALIST CONFISCATION ACTS.

(From H. Scobell's "Acts and Ordinances of the Parliament." London, 1658. Second Part.)

1651. Cap. 10.
Lands and Estates forfeited for Treason, to be sold.

a   Whereas the Estates of sir John Stowel late of Cudderstone in the [156] County of Somerset Knight of the Bath, George Duke of Buckingham, John Earl of Bristol, George Lord Digby, William Earl of Newcastle, sir William Widdrington late of Widdrington Castle in the County of Northumb. Knight, sir Philip Musgrave of Cadwel in the County of Cumberland Baronet, sir Marmaduke Langdale late of North Dalton in the County of York Knight, sir Richard Greenvile late of Stowe in the County of Cornwal Knight, sir Francis Doddington late of Barrow in the County of Somerset Knight, sir John Culpepper late of Hollingborn in the County of Kent Knight, sir John Byron
b late of Newsted-Abby in the County of Notingham Knight, Edward Earl of Worcester, sir John Winter late of Lidney in the County of Gloucester Knight, Matthew Boynton late of Scarborough in the County of York Esq; sir Lewis Dives late of Bromham in the County of Bedford Knight, Thomas Levison late of Wolverhampton in the County of Stafford Esq; James Earl of Derby, John Marquess of Winchester, sir Ralph Hopton late of Wittham in the County of Somerset Knight of the Bath, sir George Ratcliff late of Colton in the County of the City of York Knight, Francis Lord Cottington, sir Edward Harbert late of Parsons-Green in the Parish of Fulham in
c the County of Middlesex Knight, Edward Hide late of Purton in the County Wilts Esq; otherwise called sir Edward Hide, Richard Lane late of Kingsthorp in the County of Northampton Esq; deceased, otherwise called sir Richard Lane, Robert Long late of the City of Westminster Esq; Thomas Tilsley late of Myerscow in the County of

a Lancaster Esq; James Earl of Castlehaven, Philip Cartaret Esq; Son and Heir of Sir Philip Cartaret Knight deceased, John Bodvile late of   in the county of   Esq; Peter Pudsey of St. Huton [Sheriff Hutton] in the County of York Gent. James Bunch late Alderman of the City of London, sir Edward Nicholas late of the City of Westminster Knight, Marmaduke Roydon late of the City of London Merchant deceased, sometimes called sir Marmaduke Roydon, John Stowel and Edward Stowel, Esqs; sons of the said sir John Stowel, Marmaduke Langdale Esq; son of the said sir Marmaduke Langdale, Thomas Earl of Cleveland, Thomas Lord Went-
b worth eldest son of the said Earl of Cleveland, Charls Townley late of Nockton in the County of Lincoln Esq; sir Piercy Harbert son of the Lord Powys, George Benion late of Mussel-Hill in the County of Middlesex Esq; otherwise called sir George Benion, sir Henry Slingsby of Redhouse in the County of York Baronet, William Kains of Roddipole in the County of Dorset Esq; sir Francis Howard [157] late of Naward [Naworth] in the County of Cumberland Knight, Thomas Haggerston late of Haggerston in the County of Northumberland Esq; otherwise called Sir Tho. Haggerston, Andrew Coggan late of Greenwich in the County of Kent Merchant, commonly called sir
c Andrew Coggan, John Robinson late of Gwersey in the County of Denbigh Gent. sir Richard Tempest late of Stella in the County of Durham Baronet, sir Thomas Riddle late of Newcastle upon Tyne Knight, sir John Marlow of Newcastle upon Tyne Knight, Edward Grey late of Chillingham in the County of Northumberland Esq; David Jenkin senior of Cowbridge in the County of Glamorgan Esq; Henry Lord Wilmot, Philip Earl of Chesterfield, John Denham late of Egham in the County of Surrey Esq; son and Heir of sir John Denham Knight deceased, late one of the Barons of the Court of Exchequer, sir Robert Hatton late of Bennyfield-Lawn
d in the County of Northampton Knight, sir Thomas Riddle the yonger, late of the Town and County of Newcastle upon Tyne Knight, sir John Somerset late of Ragland in the County of Monmouth Knight, Roger Bodenham of Rotheras in the County of Hereford Esq; sir Henry Beddinfield of   in the County of Norfolk Knight, Thomas Beckwith of Beverley in the County of York Gent. Henry Percy Esq; Christopher Lewkenor late of the Middle Temple Esq; Rowland Ayre of Hassop in the county of Derby Esq; John Gifford of Wolverhampton in the County of Stafford Esq; James late Earl of Cambridge, commonly called Duke Hamilton, William Hamilton brother of James late Earl of Cambridge, John Earl of Lodderdale [Lauderdale] in Scotland, sir Arthur Aston late

a of the city of Oxford in the county of Oxford Knight, and Cutbert Morley late of Seymour in the county of York Esq; have been and are hereby declared and adjudged to be justly forfeited by them, for their several Treasons against the Parliament and people of England.

Be it therefore Enacted, and it is Enacted by this present Parliament, and the authority thereof, That all the Manors, **Lands, Tenements** and Hereditaments, with their and every of their Appurtenances whatsoever, which they the said sir John Stowel, George **Duke of** Buckingham, John Earl of Bristol, George Lord Digby, William Earl of Newcastle, sir William Widdrington, sir Philip Musgrave, **sir Mar-**
b maduke Langdale, sir Richard Greenvile, sir Francis Doddington, **sir John Culpepper, sir John Byron,** Edward Earl of Worcester, **sir John Winter,** Matthew Boynton, **sir Lewis Dives,** Thomas Levison, James Earl of Derby, John Marquess of Winchester, sir Ralph Hopton, sir George Ratcliff, Francis Lord Cottington, sir Edward Harbert, sir Edward Hide, Richard Lane, Robert Long, Thomas Tilsley, James Earl of Castlehaven, Philip Cartaret, John Bodvile, Peter Pudsey, James Bunch, sir Edward Nicholas and Marmaduke Roydon sometimes called sir Marmaduke Roydon, John Stowel, Edward Stowel, Marmaduke Langdale, Thomas Earl of Cleveland, Thomas Lord Wentworth,
c Charls Townley, sir Percy Harbert, **sir George Benion, sir Henry** Slingsby, sir Francis Howard, William **Kains, sir Thomas Haggerston,** Andrew Coggan, commonly called sir **Andrew Coggan, John Robinson,** sir Richard Tempest, **sir Thomas Riddle, sir John Marlow,** Edward Grey, David Jenkin, Henry Lord Wilmot, Philip Earl of **Chesterfield,** John Denham, **sir Robert Hatton,** sir Thomas Riddle **the yonger, sir John Somerset, Roger** Bodenham, **sir** Henry Beddingfield, **Thomas** Beckwith, Henry Percy, Christopher Lewkenor, Rowland **Aire,** John Gifford, James late **Earl** of Cambridge, commonly called Duke Hamilton, William Hamilton, John Earl of Lodderdale, [Lauderdale], sir
d **Arthur Aston** and Cutbert Morley, or any of **them,** or any for their use, or in trust for any of them, were seised or possessed of, in Possession, Reversion or Remainder, **on** the Twentieth day of May, One thousand six hundred forty two, **or** at any time since, and all Rights **of Entry** in or to the said Manors, Lands, Tenements or Hereditaments, which they or any of them had the said Twentieth day of May One thousand six hundred forty and two, **or** at any time since, be and are hereby vested, setled, adjudged and deemed **to be, and** are hereby in the real and actual possession and seisin of William Skinner, William Robinson, Sampson Sheffield, Samuel **Gooking,** Henry Sealy, William Lisle and Arthur Samuel, Esquires, and the survivors and survivor of them and their Heirs and assigns, **and** that they and the

a Survivors and Survivor of them and their Heirs, shall and may have the benefit and advantage of the said Rights of Entry unto the said Manors, Lands, Tenements and Hereditaments, and every of them, and that they, their Heirs and Assigns, shall hold all and every part and parcel of the said premises of the Manor of East Greenwich in free and common Soccage by Fealty onely, and by no other tenure or service whatsoever : Nevertheless upon trust and confidence that the said William Skinner, and other the persons aforenamed, or any five or more of them, shall have, hold and enjoy, all and singular the premises and every of them, subject to such trust and uses, as by this
b Act, or in and by authority of Parliament shall be hereafter further directed and appointed, and shall dispose of the same accordingly ; Saving to all and every person and persons, Bodies Politique and Corporate, their Heirs Successors, Executors, Administrators and Assigns, and every of them (other then the said sir John Stowel, George Duke of Buckingham, John Earl of Bristol, George Lord Digby, William Earl of Newcastle, Sir William Widdrington, sir Philip Musgrave, sir Marmaduke Langdale, sir Richard Greenvile, sir Francis Doddington, sir John Culpepper, sir John Byron, Edward [158] Earl of Worcester, sir John Winter, Matthew Boynton, sir Lewis
c Dives, Thomas Levison, James Earl of Derby, John Marquess of Winchester, sir Ralph Hopton, sir George Ratcliff, Francis Lord Cottington, sir Edward Harbert, sir Edward Hide, Richard Lane, Robert Long, Thomas Tilsley, James Earl of Castlehaven, Philip Cartaret son and heir of the said sir Philip Cartaret Knight deceased, John Bodvile, Peter Pudsey of St. Huton [Sheriff Hutton] aforesaid, James Bunch, sir Edward Nicholas, Marmaduke Roydon, deceased, sometimes called sir Marmaduke Roydon, John Stowel, Edward Stowel, Marmaduke Langdale, Thomas Earl of Cleveland, Thomas Lord Wentworth, Charls Townley, Sir Percy Harbert, son of the Lord Powys, sir George
d Benion, sir Henry Slingsby, William Kains, sir Francis Howard, sir Thomas Haggerston, Andrew Coggan, John Robinson, sir Richard Tempest, sir Thomas Riddle, sir John Marlow, Edward Grey, David Jenkin, Henry Lord Wilmot, Philip Earl of Chesterfield, John Denham, sir Robert Hatton, sir Thomas Riddle the yonger, sir John Somerset, Roger Bodenham, sir Henry Beddingfield, Thomas Beckwith, Henry Percy, Christopher Lewkenor, Rowland Aire, John Gifford, James late Earl of Cambridge, commonly called Duke Hamilton, William Hamilton, John Earl of Lodderdale [Lauderdale], sir Arthur Aston and Cutbert Morley, or any of them, and all others claiming, or to claim by, from or under them or any of them, or to the use of, or in trust for them or any of them, since the Twentieth

a day of May, One thousand six hundred forty two; and other then the Rights and Title of Dower of the respective Wife and Wives of them, or any of them) **All such Estates, Interests, Rents, Incumbrances, Charges, Rights in Law or Equity**, which they or any of them had, or ought to have had in or to the said Manors, Lands, Tenements, or Hereditaments, or any of them, before the said Twentieth day of May, One thousand six hundred forty two; as also all and every the **Estates and Interests**, given, granted, demised, allowed of or confirmed by any Act, Order or Ordinance of Parliament, or lawful authority derived from them unto any person or persons, Body *b* Politique or Corporate, who have constantly adhered, and been faithful unto this Parliament, and whose Estates have not otherwise been revoked or altered by this Parliament: If such person or persons, Bodies Politique or Corporate, their Heirs, Successors, Executors, Administrators or Assigns, do make his or their Right, Title, Interest, Claim, Demand, Charge, Incumbrance, or Estate in Law or Equity appear, and shall obtain an allowance thereof before Lislebone Long, Richard Edwards, Richard Saloway, Thomas Lister, John Dormer, Humphrey Edwards, Thomas Challenor, Henry Smith, John Corbet, William Leman, Humphrey Salwey, John Carew, Henry Martin, *c* Esqs; sir John Bourchier Knight, Luke **Robinson**, Daniel Blagrave, Francis Allein Alderman of London, William Sey, Edward Ash, Henry Nevil, Esquires; sir Henry Mildmay Knight, John Brown Esquire, sir William Constable Baronet, John Downs, Thomas Pury, William Ellis, Esquires, sir Thomas Widdrington Knight, Sergeant at Law, Nicholas Lechmere, John Trenchard, Cornelius Holland, Esquires, sir William Brereton Baronet, Edward Nevil Esquire, Edmond Prideaux Attorney General, Robert Reynolds Solicitor General, John Gurdon, Carew Raleigh, Luke Hodges, Denis Bond, John Moyle, Gregory Clement, Robert Goodwin, Esquires; Philip Lord Lisle, *d* George Thompson, Esquire, sir William Masham, Baronet, Edmund Harvey, James Challenor, James Nut, Augustine Garland, Esquires, and sir William Allanson Knight, or any five or more of them, who are hereby constituted a Committee for removing Obstructions in the sale of the said Lands, and may execute all and every the Powers and Authorities formerly granted by any Act or Ordinance of this present Parliament, to any Committee for removing Obstructions in the sale of any Lands appointed by Parliament to be sold; and they, or any five or more of them, are hereby constituted and appointed a Committee to receive such Claim in Writing, and to examine, allow, adjudge and determine the same, by such proof upon Oath, which the said Committee or any five or more of them are hereby impowered to administer, *a* or by such other ways or means as shall be required and approved of by them or any five or more of them, at or before the First day of December, Anno Dom. One thousand six hundred fifty one, whose Judgement and Determination shall by authority of this present Parliament, stand confirmed and good, according to the tenor and purport thereof; which said Judgement or Determination shall be, and may be transmitted by them, or any five or more of them, to the Trustees in this Act named, by them to be entred and observed accordingly; And the Trustees, Treasurers, Register-Accomptant and Surveyor-General named in this Act, and all other persons imployed *b* in or about the said Service, are required to observe such Orders and Directions as from time to time they shall receive from the said Committee: And the said Committee shall and may allow all incident Charges for the necessary carrying on of the said Service.

And for the better encouragement and security of such person or [159] persons as shall be Purchasers of the said Lands, Be it Enacted, Ordained and Declared by the Authority aforesaid, That the said William Skinner, and other the persons before named as Trustees, the Survivors and Survivor of them, and the Heirs of the Survivor of them, shall stand and be seized of all and singular the said premises, vested *c* and setled in them and their heirs (excepting Rectories Impropriate, Parsonages Impropriate, Tythes, Composition for Tythes, Portions of Tythes, Donatives, Oblations, Obventions, and Rents issuing out of Tythes) until the Estate and Conveyance thereof shall be made unto any person or persons, Body Politique or Corporate, as shall be Purchasor or Purchasers thereof, or of any part thereof, for the paying and satisfying the respective Lenders within this Act, and unto such further use and uses as shall be declared by Parliament.

And be it further Enacted by the Authority aforesaid, That the said persons aforementioned as Trustees, or any five or more of them, shall *d* have power and authority to make, nominate and appoint from time to time, by writing under their hands and seals, fit and able persons, such as they shall think fit, to survey the premises in any County or Counties of England or Wales, or in the Isle of Jersey, or Town of Berwick upon Tweed, who are hereby enabled and authorized to keep Courts of Survey for the better discovery of the premises, and the value thereof; and to pursue such further Instructions as shall be appointed from time to time by the Parliament, or such as shall be authorized thereunto.

INSTRUCTIONS FOR THE SURVEYORS.

I. That the said Trustees, or any three or more of them, shall have *a* power, and are hereby authorized to send to the Clerk to the Commissioners for Compounding, for a Particular of all and singular the Manors, Lands and Estates now under sequestration, lately belonging to all and every the Traitors in this Act named respectively; together with the Counties and Parishes, or Towns where the same do lie, and the yearly Rent for which the same are now let, which Particular the said Clerk is hereby required to make and deliver.

II. That out of the said Particular the said Trustees, or any three or more of them, shall cause an Abstract to be made of the particular Manors, Lands and Estates, of all or any the said Delinquents in each *b* County.

III. That the said Trustees, or any three or more of them, shall appoint and make choice of so many fit and able persons experienced in the mystery of Surveying, as shall be necessary for the surveying of the premises, and appoint unto them what and how many Counties they shall intermeddle with, proportioning the same so, as may best facilitate and expedite the work with least burthen to the Commonwealth; and setting down unto each of them a certain time for the return of the Surveys within the respective Counties within their Instructions, according to the quantities of the premises lying within *c* such Counties so by them to be surveyed, which Returns the said Surveyors are to make by the time limited accordingly.

IV. That the said Surveyors, or any three of them, shall have full power and authority to enter into, and survey all or any of the premises, or any part thereof lying within the respective Counties so allotted unto them, as well by the Oathes of good and lawful men, as by all other lawful ways and means to enquire and finde out all and every other Manors, Lordships, Granges, Messuages, Lands, Tenements, Meadows, Leasowes, Pastures, Woods, Rents, Reversions, Services, Parks, Annuities, and other Possessions, Priviledges, Liber-
d ties, Immunities and Hereditaments whatsoever, of what nature or quality soever they be, lying within every such County or Counties, or any City, Town, Borough or Place, within such County or Counties, which lately, or at any time since the twentieth day of May, One thousand six hundred forty two, did belong unto any Traytor or Traytors in this Act particularly named, or to any other person or persons in trust for him, them or any of them, and how much thereof is in Possession, Reversion, or Remainder, and the true yearly value thereof; and what Estates thereof now in being, were granted before the said twentieth day of May, One thousand six hundred forty two; And what Rents, Services and other Duties are reserved and payable, during such Estate, or issuing out of the same; and also what of the

a promises are chargeable to and with any good, pious and charitable use or uses; and also to enquire and survey what Timber, Buildings, open Quarries and Mines are upon the premises, and to make two particular Surveys and Certificates of their proceedings.

V. That the said Surveyors or any three of them, shall have power to keep Courts of Survey within any of the said Manors and premises, and to call before them the Tenants, and other persons who claim any Interest in the premises, to shew their Writings and Evidences, and discover what Right, Title or Interest they or any of them have or may claim of, in, to, or out of the same, or any part thereof; and also [160] *b* to examine upon Oath any person or persons (other than such as have or claim to have any Interest or Title therein) for or concerning the discovery of the Contents, Meets, Bounds, Extents, Title, Rents, Improvements, Valuations, and Jurisdictions of all or any of the Premises, and for the discovery of any Records, Evidences, or Writings concerning the same; and that the said Surveyors or any three or more of them, have hereby power to administer an Oath for the purposes aforesaid.

VI. That the said Surveyors or any three or more of them shall return one of the said Surveys to the said Trustees, and the other to *c* the Register nominated and appointed by this Act, together with all Records, Evidences and Writings concerning the same.

VII. That no Surveyor or any his Childe or Children, or any in trust for him or them, shall be admitted to be a Purchaser of any part of the Lands and Premises surveyed or to be surveyed by himself, upon pain of losing his or their purchase money, and the purchase to be void.

VIII. That the said Trustees or any five of them, do take a due Accompt of the Surveyors discharge of their Duties, and have power, in case of Neglect or Unfaithfulness, to put out such Surveyor, and to *d* put another fit person in his room.

IX. That the said Surveyors shall each of them, before he shall take upon him the execution of the said Office, take before any three of the said Trustees (who have hereby power to administer the same) the Oath following; viz.

I A.B. do swear, That I will faithfully and truly, according to my best skill and knowledge, execute the place of Surveyor, according to the purport of an Act of this present Parliament, entituled, *An Act for the sale of several Lands and Estates, forfeited to the Commonwealth for Treason;* and according to the Instructions thereunto added, I shall use my best endeavor and skill to discover the Estate therein mentioned, and every part thereof which shall be given me in Charge,

a and to finde out the true values and improvements thereof, and thereof shall make true Surveys according to my best skill and cunning; and the same from time to time to deliver in Writing close sealed up, unto Ralph Darnal Esq; the Register in that behalf appointed; together with a true Copy or Duplicate thereof, likewise close sealed up, to the said Trustees or any two of them, according to the true intent and meaning of the said Act: And this I shall justly and faithfully execute without any Gift or Reward, directly or indirectly, from any person or persons whatsoever, Except such Allowances as the said Trustees or the major part of them shall think fit to make unto me,
b for my pains and charges, in the executing of the said Place or Office.

And all Sheriffs, Majors, Bayliffs, Justices of the Peace, and other persons, are hereby required to be aiding and assisting to the said Surveyors and every of them, in the execution of this Act. And the said Surveyors are hereby authorized to demand, require, receive, and put in safe custody the Charters, Deeds, Books, Accompts, Rolls, Writings and Evidences that concern the premises or any part thereof, to the end the same may be put in such place as the said Trustees, or any five or more of them shall appoint. And the said Trustees or any five or more of them, are hereby authorized from time to time, to call
c to accompt any Surveyor or Surveyors, or other Officers by them named and appointed: And if they shall finde them or any of them deficient or unfaithful in pursuance of the duty or trust in them reposed, by unnecessary delay, or otherwise, that then they shall and may remove them or any of them which they shall so finde deficient or unfaithful, and nominate and appoint others in their stead.

And it is further Enacted, That the said Trustees, or any five or more of them, are hereby authorized to take unto them such Council Learned, and to appoint other Officers, as any five or more of them shall think necessary, and to give such Fees, and make such Allow-
d ances to them or any of them, as shall be approved of by the Committee herein named.

And it is further Enacted, That the said Trustees or any five or more of them, shall observe and pursue such Instructions as they shall receive from time to time from the Parliament, or such as shall by them be authorized thereunto.

And it is further Enacted, That the said William Skinner, William Robinson, Sampson Sheffield, Samuel Gooking, Henry Sealy, William Lisle and Arthur Samuel, or any five or more of them, shall have power and authority, and are hereby impowered and authorized, to Treat, Contract and agree, with any person or persons, Body Politique or Corporate, for the sale of the Premises or any part thereof, upon *a* such Particular or Certificate and value, as shall be delivered in unto them under the hand of the Register or his Deputy, as hereafter shall be by this Act nominated and appointed.

Provided, That the said Trustees shall not Treat or Contract with any person or persons, Body Politique or Corporate, other then the immediate Tenant or Tenants of the said Delinquents Lands, for the respective Lands, Tenements, or Hereditaments, which he or they so [163][1] hold, for the space of thirty days, to be accompted from the return of the Survey thereof. And in case such tenant or tenants do not agree, contract and subscribe his or their Contract within the said thirty *b* days, that then the said Trustees may proceed to the sale thereof to any person or persons, Body Politique or Corporate whatsoever.

And it is further Enacted, That the said Trustees shall not sell any of the Lands, Possessions, or Hereditaments of the said Traytors in Possession under ten years purchase: And the said Trustees shall not sell a Reversion of the said Lands and Hereditaments upon a Lease for one life, under five years purchase: And that a Reversion of such Lands and Hereditaments upon a Lease for two lives, shall not be sold under three years Purchase: And that a Reversion of the said premises upon a Lease for three Lives, shall not be sold under two *c* years Purchase: And where any tenant or tenants of any of the premises, claim a Right to have a Customary Estate in Reversion, or by the Custom may grant or make Leases for Life or Lives, the Reversion shall be sold proportionably to this Rate: And the said Trustees shall not sell a Reversion of the said premises upon a Lease for seven years, under five years and an half Purchase: And that a Reversion upon a Lease for fourteen years, shall not be sold under three years and an half Purchase: and that a Reversion upon a Lease for one and twenty years shall not be sold under two years, and an half Purchase: And all other Reversions upon Leases for more or *d* fewer years, shall be sold proportionable to this Rate.

And it is further Enacted, That the said Trustees named in this Act, shall take the Oath hereafter expressed, before the Lords Commissioners for the Great Seal of England, or one of them; viz. I A.B. do swear, That I will, according to my best skill and knowledge, faithfully discharge the Trust committed unto me, in relation to an Act of Parliament, Entituled, *An Act for the Sale of several Lands and Estates forfeited to the Commonwealth for Treason:* And that I will not for favour or affection, reward or gift, or hopes of reward or gift, break the same.

---

[1] There is an error in the paging of the original.

Instructions for the Trustees.

a They shall peruse all Surveys returned and to be returned of the said Lands and premises, and amend upon due proof before them upon Oath, all mistakes in Misnomer of any person or persons, places or things, and likewise without Oath to amend all other Misprisions in miscasting the Total of any particular sum of Money, or number of Acres, or such other like mistakes; and also make such Amendments in Surveys returned, and insert such words of course in Particulars or Conveyances, as they shall think fit or necessary to pass such Estates *b* as they shall Contract for to the Purchasers, according to the true intent and meaning of the Contracts which they shall make; And shall be impowered to Order and Direct the respective Surveyors to review or amend any Surveys returned, as they shall see cause; and also to add by way of Supplements to Certificates of any Estates which shall be made to appear to them.

And for the better carrying on of the said service, Be it Enacted and Ordained by the Authority aforesaid, That Ralph Darnal Esq; shall be Register, and shall have the custody and keeping of all Records, Charters, Evidences, Court-Rolls, Legerbooks, Writings, *c* Books of Survey, Certificates, and other things of or concerning the Lands and Possessions of the said Traytors, or other the premises, and shall follow such Directions and Instructions as shall be given by Parliament.

Instructions to be observed by the Register.

I. That he do receive all Surveys and Certificates to be returned by the Surveyors, and immediately after the return thereof, fairly Enter and Register the same in Books to be kept by him for that purpose, and in an orderly maner File, Bundle up, and safely keep the *d* Originals.

II. That he do weekly or oftner, certifie to the Trustees, what Surveys and Certificates are returned to him, and of what Manors or otherwise, as the case shall require.

III. That upon Warrant from the Trustees, he do make forth and fairly engross in Parchment, particulars of all such Manors, Lands, Tenements and Hereditaments, Buildings, Woods, and other things surveyed and certified into his Office by the Surveyors; Whereupon the Trustees are to proceed, or intend to make any sale, after that the same Surveys shall be allowed of by the Surveyor-General (to whom the Register and Trustees are within three days after the return of such Survey, to send the same for that purpose) and that he do *a* examine and signe the said Particulars, and deliver them to the Trustees.

IV. That upon Contracts or Agreements made by the Trustees, for any the Manors, Lands, Tenements, Hereditaments, Buildings, Woods, or other things contained in any Particular made forth, signed and delivered unto them by the Register, the said Particular be returned [164] to the Register, together with the Order of Agreement, and Contract made with the Purchaser thereupon.

V. That upon return thereof, he do forthwith rate the Particular, and ascertain the Purchase-Moneys, how much it comes to, and at how *b* many years purchase the Particulars contracted for are sold, and enter the same upon the same Particular; together with such other proceedings as shall be required by the Contract.

VI. That he do return the Particulars thus Rated and Ascertained, to the Trustees, who are to sign the same, to attest the Agreement, and thereupon to draw up and seal Conveyances thereof to the Purchasers accordingly.

VII. That all Particulars thus finished, together with all proceedings thereupon, be fairly Entered or Registered by the said Register, and be safely kept by him as Records; And that after such Entring *c* and Registring thereof, the Register do deliver the said Particulars unto the Trustees, to perfect the sale as aforesaid.

VIII. That he do weekly make Certificate to the Treasurer, Comptroller and Register-Accomptant, of all Rates of Particulars, and of all Moneys payable upon any Contract upon any Particular, how much thereof is to be paid in hand, and how much to be forborn, and for what time, and how and in what maner the sum or sums to be forborn are to be secured.

IX. That the said Register and his Deputy respectively, before they shall execute the said respective Offices, shall take before three *d* of the said Trustees, the Oath hereafter following, which the said Trustees or any three of them, have hereby power to administer; viz.

You shall well and truly execute the Office and place of Register, for the sale of several Lands and Estates forfeited to the Commonwealth for Treason, according to the Act of Parliament, and Instructions in that behalf made, and not for fear, favor, malice or reward, violate the Trusts in you reposed.

The like Oath *Mutatis mutandis* for the Deputy-Register: And the said Register shall have and receive the yearly Salary of One hundred pounds, payable upon the first day of March, and the first day of September, by equal Portions, out of the Receipts, Rents, and *a* Revenues arising out of the premises, by the hands of the Treasurers thereof, which the said Treasurers are hereby authorized and required to pay accordingly ; and the Acquittance of the said Register shall be a good discharge to the said Treasurers and every of them, for the payment thereof: And that the said Register shall have such other Fees for Writing, Rating, and Signing the said Particulars and otherwise, in the Execution of the said Office, as shall be allowed of by the Committee herein named.

And be it further Enacted by the Authority aforesaid, That the said Trustees, or any five or more of them, shall have power and *b* authority, and are hereby impowered, authorized and required to convey the premises or any part thereof, by Bargain and Sale, Inrolled according to the Statute, or otherwise by good and sufficient Conveyance and Assurance in the Law, to any person or persons whatsoever, according to such Contract or Contracts as shall be made by the said Trustees or any five or more of them : And that all Bargains of Sale, Conveyances and Assurances made of any Estate or Estates in Fee-simple, according unto such Contracts as shall be agreed upon between the Purchaser or Purchasers, and the said Trustees before named, or any five or more of them, shall be good and effectual in *c* Law, to all intents and purposes. And all and every Purchaser or Purchasers of the premises or any part thereof, his Heirs and Assigns, shall have, hold and enjoy the premises that shall be by him or them purchased, discharged of all trusts and accompts whereunto the said Trustees are or may be lyable by vertue of this present Act ; and of all suits and questions that may arise or be moved upon pretence of Sale at under-values, and all other claims and demands whatsoever ; and of all incumbrances made by the said Trustees, or by any claiming under them or any of them ; And that the said premises shall not be lyable unto, but stand, and shall be free and discharged of and from *d* all and all maner of Statutes, Judgments, Recognizances, Dowers, Jointures, and other Acts and Incumbrances whatsoever, had, made, done or suffered, or to be had, made, done or suffered, by, from or under the said Trustees, other then such Conveyances and Assurances as shall be by them had, made, done or suffered, in performance and pursuance of the Sales and Contracts respectively made, according to the intent of this present Act. And if any Action shall be brought against the said Trustees or Treasurers, or any of them, for any act done by them or any of them, in execution of this Act or Instructions, unto which it relates, or against any Purchaser or Purchasers of any of the premises, hereby appointed to be sold, his or their Heirs and Assigns, Then he or they are hereby enabled to plead the General *a* Issue, and to give this Act in Evidence; and if a Judgement pass for them, they shall recover double costs.

And whereas the Parliament do finde it necessary to raise a considerable sum of Money for the necessary carrying on the Services of this Commonwealth, Be it therefore enacted and ordained, and it is enacted and ordained, That the sum of two hundred and fifty thousand [165] pounds shall be borrowed upon the Security of the Lands of the said Traytors, by way of doubling the like sum, as is or shall be due unto any person or persons, Bodies Politique or Corporate, upon the Publique Faith; or which might have been doubled by vertue of any *b* Act, Order or Ordinance of this present Parliament, and hath not formerly been doubled upon the Credit of Bishops, or Deans and Chapters Lands: And that all and every person and persons, Bodies Politique or Corporate, for every sum of Money he or they shall further lend, may and shall be secured the Moneys formerly owing as aforesaid; And such other Moneys as he or they shall advance for the raising Two hundred and fifty thousand pounds, upon the Lands of the said Delinquents in this Act named: As for example, If there be owing to any person or persons, Body Politique or Corporate, One hundred pounds principal Money, for which he or they are to have *c* Interest, which together with Interest due thereupon, for Three years, will make One hundred twenty four pounds, he or they advancing One hundred twenty four pounds, may and shall be secured Two hundred forty eight pounds as aforesaid, and so proportionable for a greater or a lesser sum. And for the more speedy reimbursing of such Lenders, the Lands as aforesaid of the said Traytors in this Act named, are estated and vested in the said Trustees for the speedy sale thereof: And the said trustees are hereby impowered and authorized, to pursue the Rules and Instructions for doubling of Money, as is appointed and declared in the several Acts of this Parliament for the *d* sale of Dean and Chapters Lands.

And it is further enacted, That Sir John Wollaston Knight and Alderman of the City of London, Thomas Andrews, John Dethick, and Francis Allein, Aldermen of the said City, shall be Treasurers for the said Service; And that they or any two of them, are hereby impowered and authorized to receive the said Two hundred and fifty thousand pounds; and all other sum or sums of Money, as from time to time ought to be paid in to the Treasury by vertue of this Act, which shall be issued out and paid according to such Rules and Instructions, as from time to time they shall receive from the Parliament.

Instructions for the Treasurers.

I. The said Treasurer shall not issue out, or pay any part or parcel of the said two hundred and fifty thousand pounds, to be advanced by way of doubling, to any person or persons whatsoever, but according to such Orders, Directions and Instructions, as they shall from time to time have and receive from the Parliament; and that then **the Receipt of the** person or persons authorized to receive the same, **shall be a good** and sufficient discharge to the Treasurers.

II. That the said Treasurers or any two of them, after their Receipts of the Register-Accomptants Certificate, named in the said Act, of what Principal and Interest is due to any person or persons, Body Politique or Corporate, who shall be Lenders within the intent of this Act; They shall, and are hereby authorized to give such person or persons a Receipt or Receipts, as well for the old Debt and Interest, stated and certified as aforesaid, as also for the Moneys lent towards the Advancement of the said two hundred and fifty thousand pounds; And the Receipt and Receipts given by the said Treasurers, or any two of them as aforesaid, shall be a good and sufficient Authority for such person or persons, Body Politique or Corporate, their Executors, Administrators and Assigns, to require payment of the sum therein mentioned, together with Interest after the rate of six pounds *per Centum*, out of the issues and profits of the premises; and in case of failer thereof, to be allowed him or them, their Assignee or Assignes, in the purchase of the said premises or any part thereof.

And it is further Enacted, That Robert Manwaring Esq; shall be and is hereby constituted and appointed Register-Accomptant for the said service, who shall pursue such Instructions as shall be appointed from time to time by the Parliament, or such as shall by them be authorized thereunto.

Instructions for the Register-Accomptant.

The said Register-Accomptant is hereby authorized, upon the Bills, Receipts or Certificates given by any Committee (where by Ordinance of Parliament they are impowered to give the Publique Faith) or from Treasurers, Receivers or Collectors of Money, Plate, **Arms**, Horses, **with** their Furniture or **Arms**, advanced on the Publique Faith, to ascertain the Principal and Interest thereof, **and** the same to certifie unto the Treasurers or any two of them. Provided, **That** the said Register-Accomptant do not allow of any **Receipt**, Certificate or Bill of Publique Faith, but such as shall be **allowed by** the Trustees named in this Act, or any **five or more** of them, who are from time to a time to observe such Orders, Directions, and Instructions as they shall have and receive from the Parliament concerning the premises.

And be it further Enacted, That John Baker Gent. be Surveyor-General of all the said premises, who is hereby authorized, enabled and required to observe such Instructions for the Surveyor-General, as shall be appointed from time to time by the Parliament, or such as shall be by them authorized thereunto.

Instructions for the Surveyor-General.

I. The said Surveyor-General shall within six days next after he
b shall receive any of the said Surveys from the said Trustees and Register peruse them, and shall return them back to the Trustees and Register, with his Allowance and Approbation thereupon, if he finde them fit for a Purchaser to proceed upon; after which the Register shall and may make out a Particular of the whole Survey for the Purchaser to contract upon.

II. If the Surveyor-General shall finde the Surveys insufficient for to contract upon, that then he shall within six days after receipt thereof, transcribe so much of the said Survey as is imperfect, and return the same unto the respective Surveyors, and certifie them the
c causes of his Exceptions, who are hereby enjoyned forthwith to amend the same; But if they cannot, then to certifie him the cause why they cannot amend the same: And notwithstanding the Imperfection, the said Surveyor-General is to return the Surveys to the Trustees and Register, so that the immediate Tenants of any part of the premises expressed in the Survey that is imperfect, may proceed to purchase.

III. The said Surveyor shall and may, with the consent of three of the Trustees, rectifie and amend mistakes, errors and other matters that are not of substance in any of the said Surveys: And in all cases where the said Surveyor-General can by proof of Witnesses upon
d Oath (which he hath hereby power to administer) amend any Survey, without any return of the Surveyor; that then he, with the advice and consent of three of the Trustees, shall and may amend the same.

And it is further Enacted and Ordained, That none of the said Trustees, or any other, to their or any to his or their use or uses, or in trust for them or any of them, directly or indirectly, shall or do purchase the said premises, or any part thereof: And if any of the said Trustees, or any in trust for them, or any of them shall purchase any of the said premises, he and they shall forfeit his or their Estate so purchased, and the moneys paid or to be paid for the same.

And be it Enacted and Ordained by the Authority aforesaid, That the Trustees mentioned in this Act, shall have and receive two pence

a in the pound for all such Lands, Tenements and Hereditaments of the said Delinquents, which shall be contracted for and sold by them, and conveyed according to the Rates for which they shall be sold; Provided, That the said Deduction be made according as the Purchaser pays in or defalks his Purchase-money, and not otherwise: And that the Register-Accomptant shall have for his fee, the sum of One hundred pounds *per annum* added to his former Salary in his imployment of Dean and Chapters Lands; and that upon determination of that Imployment, he have two hundred pounds *per annum* for executing the Office of Register-Accomptant of the said premises, payable
b out of the Rent and Proceed of the said premises by the Treasurers thereof for the time being, on the first of March and first of September, by equal portions: And the said Register-Accomptant shall have and imploy such Clerks under him, as the Committee of Obstructions shall approve of, who shall have such Salary as the said Committee shall think fit, which shall be paid unto them in such maner as by their Order shall be set down and appointed: And that the Surveyor-General shall have for his Fee, for him and his Clerks, for the said service, the sum of One hundred pounds *per annum*, payable out of the Rents and Proceeds of the said premises by the Treasurers thereof
c for the time being, on the first of March, and the first of September, by equal Portions.

And be it further Enacted and Ordained by the Authority aforesaid, That all and every Body Politique and Corporate, shall have power and authority, and are hereby Enabled, to take and purchase to themselves and Successors, any of the said Manors, Lands, Tenements and Hereditaments, to themselves, their Heirs and Successors for ever, without suing forth any License or Licenses of Alienation or Mortmain, any Law, Statute or Charter to the contrary in any wise notwithstanding.

d And be it further Ordained, Enacted and Declared by the authority aforesaid, That all and every person and persons, Body Politique and Corporate, who shall Contract for any of the said premises, shall pay in, or defalk the first Moyety of his or their Purchase-moneys within Eight weeks after his Contract made; and shall likewise prosecute or procure his or their respective Conveyances from the said Trustees appointed to convey the premises within the said Eight weeks, or otherwise he or they shall forfeit the third part of the whole Moneys payable upon his or their respective Contracts, unless he or they can procure from the said Trustees, or any five or more of them, upon [167] good cause shewn and to be allowed by them, a Certificate or Certificates for further time to perfect his or their Conveyance, which *a* Certificate and further License or Licenses as aforesaid, the said Trustees are hereby authorized to give.

And be it further Enacted, and it is further Enacted by the Authority aforesaid, That the said Trustees named in this Act, for the Conveying the said premises, and the Purchaser and Purchasers of all or any the said Manors, Lands, Tenements or Hereditaments, belonging to the said Traytors, their and every of their respective Heirs and Assigns, shall have, hold, use and enjoy the like Benefits, Priviledges, Rights, Usages, and Customs; and likewise take all Advantages, Benefits of Conditions broken, Forfeitures or Non-per-
b formance of Covenants, Entries or Actions, as the said respective Traytors might have done, or ought to have had or enjoyed.

And be it further Enacted, That Randal Manwaring Esq; shall be Comptroller of all Entries, Receipts and Payments which shall be made to or by the said Treasurers, and shall have Power and Authority, by himself or his sufficient Deputies, to keep Accompt of all Entries, Receipts, Payments and Discounts whatsoever, which shall be made unto, or by the said Treasurers: And the said Comptroller or his Deputies shall execute the said place of Comptroller in relation to the premises, according to such Instructions and Directions as are given to
c the Comptroller for the Receipts of Bishops Lands, by an Ordinance of Parliament of the sixteenth of November, One thousand six hundred forty six, and shall receive the like Fee and Salary, and quarterly Payments, as the Comptroller appointed by the said Ordinance ought to have done.

Instructions for the Comptroller.

I. The Comptroller by himself or his sufficient Deputies, shall attend daily, according to the usual times, and be present at Receipts
d and Payments made within the said Treasurers Office, and make Duplicates or Entries of the same in fitting Books to be provided and kept for that purpose.

II. That every Purchaser, upon every payment of any sum of Money that he shall make to the Treasurer, shall enter his Acquitance with the Comptroller, which the said Comptroller is to enter without Fee.

III. That the said Treasurers or their Clerk to the Cash, shall weekly upon every Monday morning deliver the Comptroller or his Deputy, a Copy of all Receipts, Payments and Disbursements, and to whom, during the preceding Week, which the Comptroller is hereby required to enter into a Book to be kept for that purpose; and that *a* no payment to be made by the said Treasurers shall be allowed upon their Accompt, unless an Accompt be weekly given as aforesaid.

IV. That the Register shall weekly upon every Monday make Certificate to the Comptroller of all Rates of Particulars, and of all moneys payable upon any such Particulars, Contracts or Bargains made by vertue of the said Act, which shall be forborn upon Security; and how and by whom the same is secured, and at what time payable, which Certificate the Comptroller shall enter in a Book to be kept by him for that purpose: And likewise in the moyety of the Purchase-money (for so much as the same shall be estimated by the Register, *b* in case it cannot be ascertained) at such time as the Trustees Certificate shall appoint; and also agree to pay the second moyety within six moneths after such payment of the first. Provided, That if the aforesaid estimate of the Moyety of the Purchase-money paid in as aforesaid, shall upon casting up of the Rates appear to be more or less then the true Moyety of the said Purchase-money, that then there shall be such abatement or addition out of, or unto the second payment, as shall reduce and bring it to the just Moyety. And it is hereby Enacted and Ordained, That the forfeitures of all such persons who have any moneys secured unto them by this Act, shall be wholly *c* defalked by the Treasurers out of such moneys, if the same be sufficient to satisfie the same; and if not, then the said Treasurers are to detain so much as is due unto them upon the said Security to be raised, and the residue of the said moneys so forfeited, as is hereafter directed: And such person and persons who have no moneys so secured, and notwithstanding shall contract for the premises or any part thereof, and shall not perfect his or their Conveyance by the time aforesaid, his or their forfeiture shall be levied as in this Act hereafter is directed. And it is further Enacted and Ordained, That such person or persons as shall incur or make any forfeiture as aforesaid, shall pay *d* in to the Treasurers his or their moneys so forfeited, or so much of it as is unsatisfied, within ten days next after such forfeiture made; and in default thereof, the said Treasurers are hereby required, under their Hands to certifie such neglects of non-payment unto the Trustees, within three days next after such default made: And thereupon the said Trustees or any five of them, are hereby required and enjoyned to make Certificate under their hands, of the sum or sums of money forfeited as aforesaid, unto the Sub-commissioners for Sequestrations, in the respective Counties where such person or persons forfeiting as aforesaid, have or hath any real or personal Estate: And the said respective Sub-Commissioners shall, and are hereby authorized and required, upon the receipt of such Certificate [168]

a from the said Trustees to Seize and Sequester the real and personal Estate of such person or persons so forfeiting as aforesaid, and the same to detain in their Custody, without sale or disposal thereof, for the space of ten days: And if the said person or persons so Sequestred do pay or cause to be paid in to the said Treasurers, his or their forfeiture within the ten days, that then upon Certificate thereof from the said Treasurers or any two of them, to the said Sub-Commissioners, the said Sub-Commissioners shall discharge the Sequestration of the said real and personal Estate of such person or persons: But in default of such Payment to the said Treasurers
b within the said ten days, then the said Sub-Commissioners are hereby authorized and required to levy and raise such sum and sums of Money so certified unto them as aforesaid, by sale of the Goods, and Receipt of the Rents, Issues and Profits of the Lands of such person or persons; And after the said sum so raised, the Lands and Residue of the said Goods to be restored and discharged from Sequestration. And it is hereby Enacted and Ordained, That all and every the said Forfeitures so to be raised by the said respective Sub-Commissioners, shall be paid in by them to the said Treasurers, to be disposed of as other the Moneys to be raised by the said sale.
c And it is further Enacted and Ordained, That after such Forfeiture incurred, it shall and may be lawful for any five or more of the said Trustees, to contract for, and sell all or any of the said Lands so contracted for, and not prosecuted, to any other person or persons, notwithstanding the former contract, as if it never had been made.

And be it further Enacted and Ordained, That the House in the Strand, commonly called Worcester-House, or some such other place as the said Trustees shall think fitting, shall be the place where the said several and respective persons shall and may transact the said Service, and put in execution this Act.

d Provided nevertheless, That if any tenant had a good Estate before the said Twentieth day of May, One thousand six hundred forty two, and hath surrendred the same for another Estate, the said former Estate shall be allowed unto the said tenant during the continuance thereof, the said Surrender so made in any wise notwithstanding.

Provided also, That all Moneys payable by any Act, Order, or Ordinance at Goldsmiths-Hall, or to the Treasurers thereof, shall be paid as formerly, until sale shall be made of the premises, this Act or any thing therein contained to the contrary in any wise notwithstanding.

Provided always, That this Act or any thing therein contained shall not in any wise extend or be prejudicial unto, bar or take *a* away the Right, Remainder, Reversion, Title or Demand of Charls Fleetwood Esq; and Frances his Wife, or either of them, their or either of their Heirs or Assignes, of, in or to the Manor of Armingland in the County of Norfolk, or the Manor of Wisset in the County of Suffolk, or of, in or to any other Manors, Lordships, Messuages, Lands, Tenements or Hereditaments, in the Counties of Norfolk or Suffolk, or either of them, heretofore belonging to Sir Owen Smith Knight, deceased, or whereof the said Sir Owen Smith was seized.

Provided also, That if any person or persons shall double any sum of Money upon forged Debentures, or other false Certificates, or *b* any other fraudulent way or means, and thereof shall be convicted by Oath before the Committee, within one year after such Doubling, every such person so offending, shall forfeit treble the said sum, the one Moyety thereof to the use of the Commonwealth, and the other Moyety to such person or persons as shall discover the same before the said Committee in this Act named, and shall be committed to prison, and his Estate sequestred by the said Committee, until payment thereof or discharge of his Imprisonment.

Provided always, and be it further Enacted, That all and every person or persons having any Estate, Right, Title or Interest, of in *c* or unto any the Lands, Tenements or Hereditaments, by this Act intended or mentioned to be put to sale, or that hath any Statute, Judgement, Recognizance or Rent, unto which such Lands are liable; and shall make it appear unto the Committee in this Act named, That such Estate, Right, Title, Interest, Statute, Judgement, Recognizance or Rent, were without fraud, and for good and valuable consideration, had, made and acknowledged before any Treason respectively committed by any of the Traytors in this Act named; and shall obtain an allowance thereof by the said Committee, before the Nine and twentieth day of September, One thousand six hundred *d* fifty one, That then the same shall be good and effectual to such [169] person or persons, their Heirs, Executors, Administrators and Assignes respectively, to all Intents and Purposes, according to the tenor thereof, Anything in this Act to the contrary in any wise notwithstanding.

Provided always, That this Act or any thing therein contained, shall not extend to the Common-Hall or Yard, commonly called The Castle and Castle-Yard of Okeham in the County of Rutland, belonging lately to the Duke of Buckingham, which is and heretofore hath been the publique Place for the holding of the General Assizes and Sessions in that County, but be and remain for the accustomed use of the said County of Rutland.

a Provided nevertheless, and it is further Enacted, That in Recompence and Satisfaction of such Judgements, Statutes, Recognizances and other Incumbrances, as by the true Intent and Provision of this Act are to be satisfied, the said Trustees or any five or more of them, upon the return of the respective Surveys, are hereby impowered and authorized to set out such proportion of the Lands so surveyed, as will be sufficient to satisfie such Incumbrance and Incumbrances: And after such Incumbrances proved, and the Debts allowed of by the Committee in this Act named, to sell and convey such proportionable part of the said Lands so surveyed, to such Creditor or Creditors, *b* or their Assignes, in recompence and satisfaction of such Incumbrance and Incumbrances, either for life, lives, years or in Fee; the said Trustees taking care in satisfying such Incumbrances, to satisfie the same in such priority and course, as the same ought to be satisfied by the Laws of this Land: And upon such Conveyance and Conveyances made, the said Creditor and Creditors, their Heirs, Executors, Administrators or Assignes, shall acknowledge satisfaction upon Record, or otherwise release and discharge such Judgements, Statutes, Recognizances, and other Incumbrances respectively, as the Counsel of the said Trustees and for the Commonwealth, shall direct and *c* advise; And such Acknowledgement, Release and Discharge shall be good and effectual in Law to discharge the said Debts and Incumbrances, as against the residue of the Lands intended to be sold by this Act, Any Law, Statute or Usage to the contrary in any wise notwithstanding.

Provided always, and it is hereby Declared and Enacted, That this Act or any thing therein contained, shall not extend to that Capital Messuage, Farm or Tenement, known by the name of Candle-wake Court, in the Parish of Candle-wake, or Bishops Candle, both or one of them in the County of Dorset, heretofore belonging to the said *d* George Lord Digby, and John Earl of Bristol, or one of them; nor to any of the Messuages, Buildings, Lands, Tenements, and Hereditaments, to the said Farm belonging or appertaining, or taken, reputed or known, as part, parcel or member thereof, their or any of their Appurtenances; But that all the said Capital Messuage, Farm or Tenement, with all other the last mentioned premises, be, and are hereby granted, vested, setled, and established, to and upon Joan Fitz-James, daughter of Leweson Fitz-James, of Leweson in the County of Dorset Esq; deceased, and her Heirs and Assignes for ever, to the onely proper use and behoof of her the said Joan Fitz-James, her Heirs and Assignes for ever, to be held of the Manor of East-Greenwich, in Free and Common Socage by Fealty onely.

a   Provided always, and be it Enacted, That the Manor of Henden in the County of Middlesex, late the Lands of Sir Percy Herbert Knight, in the Bill mentioned, be charged with one Rent-Charge of Sixty pounds a year, during the Life of Margaret Hooker, the Relict and **Widow of** Nicholas Hooker, late Goldsmith and Citizen of London: And that the same be paid to her the said Margaret Hooker and her Assignes, upon the Four and twentieth day of June, the twenty ninth day of September, the twenty fifth of December, and upon the twenty fifth day of March, by equal portions: And in default of payment thereof, or any part thereof, the said Margaret
b shall and may from time to time distrain.

And be it further Enacted by the Authority aforesaid, That it shall and may be lawful, to and for all and every person and persons, who have and hath constantly adhered to this present Parliament, and shall prove before the Committee in this Act named, and obtain from them a Certificate, that he or they hath or have before the Tenth day of June, One thousand six hundred fifty and one, obtained a Judgement or Judgements against any of the persons whose Estates are hereby appointed to be sold, for any sum or sums of Money, Goods or Estate, forced, taken from, or plundered from such person
c or persons for adhering to the Parliament, to double all and every such sum and sums of Money, so recovered and certified by the said Committee upon this Act; and that the Trustees, Treasurers and Register-Accomptant in this Act named, do admit the same accordingly.

Provided always, That notwithstanding this Act or any thing therein contained, the sum of seven thousand pounds be satisfied to the Town of Taunton, towards the Reparations of their great losses [170] and sufferings, out of the Estate of Sir John Stowel Knight of the Bath; And that the Trustees appointed by this Act, do convey unto such Trustees as shall be named by the Mayor and Burgesses of the
d said Town, so much of the Lands of the aforesaid Sir John, by this Act exposed to sale, as shall amount unto the full value of seven thousand pounds, to be sold by the said Trustees, and the Moneys thereby raised, to be distributed according to the Votes of Parliament in that behalf.

Provided always, and be it Enacted by this present Parliament, That one Moyety in severalty of all and singular the Manors, Lands, Tenements, and Hereditaments whatsoever of Cutbert Morley in this Act named, shall by the Trustees herein before named, be conveyed and assured unto Laurence **Maidwel Esq**; and to his Heirs, the discoverer of the said Estate, or to such person or persons, and to his and their Heirs, as he shall nominate and appoint, as a Recompence for *a* the said discovery, any thing in these Presents contained to the contrary notwithstanding; And that the other Moyety of the Lands, Tenements, and Hereditaments, be by them sold and disposed of, to and for the use, benefit and behoof of the Committee of the Navy, to be by them imployed, in and about the Navy, in such maner as they shall direct and appoint, Any thing herein to the contrary notwithstanding.

Provided always, That the said Trustees shall have power to sell unto James Powel, his Heirs and Assigns, Lands to the value of One thousand and three hundred pounds, as for doubled Moneys out of the *b* Lands and Estate of Sir John Stowel in this Act named, any thing in this Act to the contrary in any wise notwithstanding.

Provided also, That this Act or any thing therein contained, do not extend to the taking away of the sum of three thousand pounds formerly conferred by the Parliament upon Margaret Rainborow, the Widow of Colonel Thomas Rainborow deceased, and upon his son William Rainborow, to be so setled out of the Estate of Richard Thornhil of Olentight in the County of Kent Esq; now Ordered to be sold; But that it may be lawful for the said Margaret, before any disposal of any part of the Estate, to purchase so much thereof, or of *c* the Estate of any other Delinquent hereby appointed to be sold, as shall amount to the said sum of three thousand pounds, according to the rate of ten years purchase for Lands in Possession, and for Lands in Reversion proportionably, allowing the said three thousand pounds upon the said Purchase as ready Money: And the Trustees and Contractors therein named, are hereby authorized and required, to contract with, and assure unto the said Margaret, to the use of her the said Margaret and her Heirs for ever, Lands, Tenements and Hereditaments, out of the said Estate, to the value of two thousand pounds at the rate aforesaid, for and towards the payment of the *d* Debts of the said Colonel Thomas Rainborow, and likewise to Contract with, Convey and Assure unto the said Margaret Rainborow, to the use of her said son William Rainborow, and the Heirs of his Body, Lands, Tenements and Hereditaments, out of the said Estate at the rate aforesaid, to the value of One thousand pounds. And in case it shall happen, that the said William Rainborow shall die without any Heirs of his Body lawfully begotten, then the said Lands, and Tenements, and Hereditaments to be to the use of the said Margaret Rainborow, and her Heirs for ever. And the Trustees and Contractors therein named, are hereby authorized and required to accept of the Discharge of the said Margaret Rainborow, under her Hand and Seal, in full satisfaction for three thousand pounds.

a Provided always, That the Trustees and Contractors in this Act named, shall and do bargain, sell and convey unto Nathaniel Hallows Esq; and his Heirs for ever, Lands and Tenements of the clear yearly value beyond Reprizes, of One hundred pounds, out of the Lands and Tenements by this Act intended and appointed to be sold, in full Compensation of One thousand pounds Debt, and his Damages, Any thing in this Act to the contrary in any wise notwithstanding.

Provided always, That after the Expiration or other Determination of a Lease made to the Lord Howard of Estrick by the Commissioners of Goldsmiths Hall, of Wallingford House, with the Appurtenances
b lying in the City of Westminster, late the Inheritance of George Duke of Buckingham in this Act named; The same shall be, and remain for ever, to the use of the Commonwealth, to be disposed as the Parliament shall order and appoint, Any thing in this Act to the contrary in any wise notwithstanding.

Provided always, That this Act shall not extend to that Copyhold-Tenement, in Froom Vawchurch in the County of Dorset, in which Lieutenant John Chaning had formerly his life; But that the Copyhold of the said Tenement be filled up with the lives of the two sons of the said Lieutenant John Chaning; And the Trustees in this
c Act named, are hereby authorized to fill up the said Copyhold as aforesaid.

Provided always, and be it Enacted by this present Parliament, [171] and by the Authority thereof, That the Trustees aforesaid in and by this Act named, upon reasonable request to them, or any four or more of them, made by Carew Raleigh Esq; son and heir of Sir Walter Raleigh Knight deceased, shall be authorized and required, of the late Lands, Tenements and Hereditaments of John Earl of Bristol, or George Lord Digby, to convey unto, and to setle upon the said Carew Raleigh and his Heirs, so much and so many Lands,
d Tenements and Hereditaments, as shall amount unto the clear yearly value of Five hundred pounds *per annum*, over and above all Reprizes, for and in full satisfaction and discharge of one yearly Pension and Annuity of Four hundred pounds *per annum*, for divers years in arrear and unpaid, and due and payable for great and valuable considerations unto the said Carew Raleigh, for the term of his natural Life, out of the Publique Exchequer, Lands and Revenues of this Commonwealth: And that for and in consideration of the said Lands and Tenements, so to be passed, conveyed and setled, to and upon the said Carew Raleigh and his Heirs, he the said Carew Raleigh shall give and pay no further or other consideration whatsoever; but the said Trustees in and by this Act named, shall pass, convey and

a settle the said Lands and Tenements, as if purchase thereof had been made by Bills transferred, or doubled moneys, according to the directions in the said Act given and appointed.

Provided always, and be it Enacted by the Authority aforesaid, That this present Act, or any thing therein contained, shall not extend unto the Manor of Pellenny, the Manors of Monmouth and Wysham, the Manors of Purcasseck and Trellects-Grange, the Manors, Castles and Demeasnes of the Manors and Castles of Grismont, St. Kenfreth, Monmouth and White-Castle, the Lands and Tenements called Bettus and Perlloyd, all which are in the County of Mon-
b mouth; nor to the Manor of Crookham in the County of Berks; nor to the Manor of Kendal in the County of Westmerland; nor to the Manors of Shobden and Poston in the County of Hereford; but that the same (the Lands reputed parcel of the said Manors of Purcasseck and Trellects-Grange, or one of them called Crymlands, formerly granted or intended to be granted in the hereafter mentioned Act to Oliver Cromwel and his Heirs onely excepted) be they Manors, Lordships, or but reputed or named Manors or Lordships; and by whatsoever name or names the same intended premises are called or known, and the Lands, Tenements and Hereditaments, being or
c reputed to be parcel of, appertaining to, or occupied or enjoyed with any of them, shall be and remain for and during the natural life onely of Edward Lord Herbert of Ragland, now called Earl of Worcester, as forfeited unto the Commonwealth; and for and during the life of the said Edward, shall and may be disposed of by vertue of this Act; and immediately from and after the death of the said Edward, or other determination of that particular Estate during his life, the same shall remain and be unto Henry called Lord Herbert, son and heir apparent of the said Edward, and unto his heirs; which said Manors and premises estimated to be of the yearly value of One thousand
d seven hundred pounds twelve shillings and ten pence, shall from henceforth as a Remainder onely, and not to take effect in possession till after the Death of the said Edward, or other Determination of the said particular Estate during his Life, be, and remain unto the said Henry called Lord Herbert, and his Heirs, in lieu and recompence of all such Right or pretence of Right, as the said Henry called Lord Herbert hath, or any his Heirs or Issues, may have, of, in or to any the Manors, Lordships, Lands, Tenements and Hereditaments herein after mentioned; that is to say, The Manors of Chalton alias Chanton, Clanfield, Catherinton and Blendworth, in the County of Southampton, with their and every of their Rights, Members and Appurtenances; the Advowsons and Rights of Patronage to the

a Churches of the Parishes of Chalton alias Chanton, Clanfield, Catherinton and Blendworth, in the said County of Southampton, and all other the Manors, Lands, Tenements, Tythes, Advowsons, Rights, Right of Action, Titles of Entry, Conditions and Hereditaments of Henry late Earl of Worcester, Edward Lord Herbert, Sir Charls Somerset, and Sir John Somerset, or any of them within the said County of Southampton; the Manors of Tydenham and Wollaston, scituate, lying and being in the County of Glocester, with their and every of their Rights, Members and Appurtenances, the Advowsons and Rights of Patronage of the Churches of the Parishes of Tydenham, Wollaston and Alvington, in the said County of Glocester;
b the several and free Fishings and Wears in the Rivers of Wye and Sovern in the said County of Glocester; the Manors and Lordships of Chepstow alias Stragul alias Struggle, Barton alias Pentherry, Hardwick, St. Kynmarks and Crymland, with their and every of their Rights, Members and Appurtenances in the County of Monmouth; the Advowsons and Rights of Patronage of the several Churches of the several Parishes of Chepstow, Pentherry, St. Arvans, New-Church and Lamsham, in the said County of Monmouth, with their and every [172] of their Rights, Members and Appurtenances, the Lands, Tenements
c and Hereditaments, called or known by the name of Chepstow-Grange, with the Rights, Members and Appurtenances thereof, in the said County of Monmouth; the Lands, Tenements and Hereditaments, called or known by the name of Fryth-wood and Barnets-wood with their and every of their Rights, Members and Appurtenances, lying and being in the Parishes, Fields and Territories of St. Arvan, Howick, Newchurch, Chepstow and Mathern, some or one of them in the said County of Monmouth; the Manors and Lordships of Magor Regis, Redwick, Moors Court, Miles Court, Marthering Ringes alias Marthingeringes-Grange, with their Rights, Members and Appurten-
d ances in the said County of Monmouth, the Advowsons and Rights of Patronage to the Churches of the several Parishes of Magor and Redwick, with their Rights, Members and Appurtenances in the County of Monmouth; and also the Manors and Lordships of Anglicana Gower, Wallicana Gower, Swansey, Kilvey, Supraboscos, Subboscos, Oystermouth, Pennard, Lougher, Kythal alias Kitle, Trewithrah alias Triveday and Lunnon alias Ilston, with their and every of their Rights, Members and Appurtenances in the County of Glamorgan; and also the Advowsons and Rights of Patronage of the Churches of the several Parishes of Gower and Swansey, with their and either of their Rights, Members and Appurtenances; All which, together with all Priviledges, Powers, Freedoms, Rights, Liberties and Immu-

a nities, granted, mentioned and expressed in one Act made this present Parliament, Entituled, *An Act for setling certain Manors, Lands and Tenements upon Oliver Cromwel, Lord Lieutenant of Ireland, and his Heirs*, are by authority of this present Act discharged of all pretence of Right, made or to be made by the said Henry called Lord Herbert.

And it is hereby Ordained and Enacted, That the said former Act stand, and be in all things ratified and confirmed; and that the said Oliver Cromwel and his Heirs and Assigns, and such person and persons to whom he hath made any Conveyance or Assurance of the *b* premises or any part thereof, since the Seventh day of February, in the year of our Lord, One thousand six hundred forty and five, according to the effect and meaning of such Conveyance, shall hold and enjoy the Manors, Lands, Tenements and Hereditaments last above mentioned, according to the said recited or mentioned Act, and with the respective Discharges, Advantages, Savings and Provisions in the said recited Act contained, and further discharged of all and every the Estate, Right, Title, Interest, Claim, Reversion, Remainder and Demand whatsoever, of him the said Lord Herbert, or of the heir or heirs of the body, or heirs males of the body, or issues of the body of *c* him the said Henry Lord Herbert; and also discharged of all such Estates, Rights, Titles, Charges, Remainders, Possibilities, Expectancies and Demands whatsoever, which he the said Henry Lord Herbert, by any common Recovery duly had against him, as Tenant or Voucher, or by any other means, could, might or may, or can cut off or bar, in case no such forfeiture had been.

And that whereas the said Henry Lord Herbert hath propounded his readiness and willingness, in respect of the said recompence, to do or consent unto any Act, for the further assuring of the premises, so as aforesaid setled upon the said Oliver Cromwel; and in pursuance *d* thereof, he the said Henry Lord Herbert hath by his Deed, under his Hand and Seal, confirmed the premises to the said Oliver Cromwel and his heirs; It is hereby further Enacted, That the same Deed of Confirmation, according to the purport thereof, shall in all things stand firm and binding unto the said Henry Lord Herbert and his heirs for ever. Saving to all and every person and persons, Bodies Politique and Corporate, their heirs and successors (other than the said Henry Earl of Worcester and Edward Earl of Worcester, Sir Charls Somerset and Sir John Somerset) and all and every person and persons having any Estate in the premises hereby setled upon the said Lord Herbert, by, from or under them or any of them since the Twentieth day of May, in the year of our Lord, One thousand six a hundred forty and one, and other then the Estate and Title accrued to the Commonwealth, All such Estate, Right, Title, Interest, as they had or might have in the premises by this present Act setled as aforesaid, upon the said Henry Lord Herbert, as if this Act had not been had or made.

Provided always, and be it further Enacted, That the Trustees in this Act named, shall bargain and sell unto George Wither Esq; his Heirs and Assigns for ever, Lands, Tenements and Hereditaments, of the clear yearly value beyond all Reprizes, of One hundred and fifty pounds out of the Estate of John Denham in this Act named, according to an Order of Parliament of the Second of January, One thousand six hundred and fifty, Anything in this Act to the contrary in any wise notwithstanding. [173]

Provided always, and be it further Enacted, That the Trustees in this Act named, shall convey unto Thomas Foxley, his Heirs and Assigns for ever, Lands, Tenements and Hereditaments, appointed by this Act to be sold, to the clear yearly value of one hundred pounds per annum, Any thing in this Act to the contrary notwithstanding.

Passed 16 *July.*

1652. Cap. 11.

Lands and Estates, forfeited by several persons, sold for the use of the Navy. [193]

a Whereas the Estates of William Lord Craven, Thomas Cook of Grays-Inn in the County of Middlesex esq; John Forcer of Haberhouse in the county of Durham, Ralph Pudsey of Stapleton in the county of Durham, Robert Blundel of Ince-Blundel in the county of Lancaster, Thomas Clifton of Litham in the county of Lancaster, Richard Massey of Rixam in the county of Lancaster, Edward Scasebrook of Scasebrook in the county of Lancaster, George Smith of Quenneborough in the county of Leicester, John Jones of Dingastow in the county of Monmouth, Lancelot Errington of East Denton in the county of Northumberland, Nicholas Errington of Pont-Island in *b* the county of Northumberland, Henry Errington of Befront in the county of Northumberland, John Lawson of St. Anthonies in the county of Northumberland, Sir Edward Ratcliff of Dilston in the county of Northumberland K^t and Baronet, Peter Gifford of Chillington in the county of Stafford, Walter Fowler of St. Thomas in the county of Stafford, Thomas Brook of Madely in the county of Salop, John Weston of Maze in the county of Surrey, Philip Hungate of Saxton in the county of York, Robert Dolman of Badsworth in the county of York, Francis Biddulph of Biddulph in the county of Stafford, Philip Anne of Burwallis in the county of York, Sir Walter Vavasor of *c* Haslewood in the county of York, William Middleton of Stockhal in the county of York, John Wiseman of Wimbish in the county of Essex esq; Henry Killigrew of Lanrack in the county of Cornwal, Sir Henry Farrar of Skillingthorp in the county of Lincoln, and Henry late Viscount Dunbar of Holderness in the county of York [194] deceased, have been, and are hereby declared and adjudged to be justly forfeited by them for their several Treasons against the Parliament and People of England; Be it therefore Enacted by this present Parliament, and the Authority thereof, That all the Manors, Lands, Tenements and Hereditaments, with their and every of their Appur-
d tenances whatsoever, which they the said William Lord Craven, Thomas Cook, John Forcer, Ralph Pudsey, Robert Blundel, Thomas Clifton, Richard Massey, Edward Scasebrook, George Smith, John Jones, Lancelot Errington, Nicholas Errington, Henry Errington, John Lawson, Sir Edward Ratcliff, Peter Gifford, Walter Fowler,

a Thomas Brook, John Weston, Philip Hungate, Robert Dolman, Francis Biddulph, Philip Anne, Sir Walter Vavasor, William Middleton, John Wiseman, Henry Killigrew, Sir Henry Farrar and Henry late Viscount Dunbar, or any of them, or any for their use or uses, or in trust for any of them, were seized or possessed of in Possession, Reversion or Remainder, on the twentieth day of May, One thousand six hundred forty two, or at any time since; And all Rights of Entry, and the whole Estates, Rights, Titles and Interests of them and every of them, in or to the said Manors, Lands, Tenements or Hereditaments, which they or any of them had the said twentieth day of May, One *b* thousand six hundred forty two, or at any time since (Excepting Rectories impropriate, Tythes, Composition for Tythes, Portions of Tythes, Donatives, Oblations, Obventions and Rents issuing out of Tythes) Be and are hereby Vested, Adjudged and Deemed to be, and are hereby in the real and actual possession and seisin of William Skinner, William Robinson, Sampson Sheffeild, Samuel Gooking, Henry Sealy, William Lisle, and Arthur Samuel, Esquires, and the Survivors and Survivor of them, and their Heirs and Assigns; And that they and the Survivors and Survivor of them and their Heirs, shall and may have the Benefit and Advantage of the said Rights of *c* Entry unto the said Manors, Lands, Tenements and Hereditaments, and every of them; And that they, their Heirs and Assigns, shall hold all and every part and parcel of the said premises of the Manor of East Greenwich, in free and common Socage by Fealty onely, and by no other Tenure or Service whatsoever: Nevertheless upon trust and confidence, that the said William Skinner and other the persons aforenamed, or any five or more of them, shall have, hold and enjoy all and singular the premises and every of them, for the onely Use and Benefit of the Navy.

Saving to all and every person and persons, Bodies Politique and *d* Corporate, their Heirs, Successors, Executors, Administrators and Assigns, and every of them (other then the said William Lord Craven, Thomas Cook, John Forcer, Ralph Pudsey, Robert Blundel, Thomas Clifton, Richard Massey, Edward Scasebrook, George Smith, John Jones, Lancelot Errington, Nicholas Errington, Henry Errington, John Lawson, Sir Edward Ratcliff, Peter Gifford, Walter Fowler, Thomas Brook, John Weston, Philip Hungate, Robert Dolman, Francis Biddulph, Philip Anne, Sir Walter Vavasor, William Middleton, John Wiseman, Henry Killigrew, Sir Henry Farrar, and Henry late Viscount Dunbar, or any of them, and all others claiming and to claim by, from or under them or any of them, since the twentieth day of May, One thousand six hundred forty two; and other then the Rights and *a* Title of Dower of the respective Wife and Wives of them or any of them) All such Estates, Interests, Rents, Incumbrances, Charges, Rights in Law or Equity, which they or any of them had or ought to have had, in or to the said Manors, Lands, Tenements or Hereditaments or any of them, before the said twentieth day of May, One thousand six hundred forty two; As also all and every the Estates and Interests given, granted, demised, allowed of or confirmed by any Act, Order or Ordinance of Parliament, or lawful Authority derived from them, unto any person or persons, Body Politique or Corporate, who have constantly adhered and been faithful to this Parliament, *b* and whose Estates have not otherwise been revoked or altered by this Parliament: If such person or persons, Bodies Politique or Corporate, their Heirs, Successors or Assigns, do before the First day of October, which shall be in the year One thousand six hundred fifty and two, deliver in writing unto the Commissioners appointed by an Act, Entituled, *An Act for transferring the Powers of the Committees for Obstructions*, or any four or more of them, a Particular of such his or their Right, Title, Interest, Claim, Demand, Incumbrance or Estate in Law or Equity, and shall obtain an Allowance thereof by the said Commissioners or any four or more of them, at or before the First day *c* of November, which shall be in the year of our Lord God, One thousand six hundred fifty and two; which said Commissioners are hereby appointed to be Commissioners for removing of Obstructions in the Sale of all and every the premises hereby appointed to be sold; And shall have, use and exercise all and every the like Powers and Authorities in reference to the premises hereby appointed to be sold, as the said Commissioners may or ought to do in relation to the sale of any other the Lands and Estates in an Act, Entituled, *An Act for Sale of several Lands and Estates forfeited to the Commonwealth for Treason*, mentioned; And the Trustees, Treasurers, Register, *d* Register-Accomptant, Surveyor-General, and all other persons im- [195] ployed in and about this service, are required to observe such Orders and Directions as from time to time they shall receive from the said Commissioners; and the said Commissioners shall and may allow all incident charges for the necessary carrying on of this service.

And the said Trustees or any five or more of them respectively, shall and may, and are hereby required and authorized to contract, bargain, sell, alien and convey, all and every the said Manors and premises, and to execute all Powers and Authorities in the sale thereof, according to the rates and Proportions, Rules and Directions limited and expressed in the said former Act for Sale of several Lands and Estates forfeited to the Commonwealth for Treason, and in such maner *a* as they may or might have done in the Sale of any the Manors or Lands vested and setled in them by the aforesaid Act: And that all and every Bargains and Sales, Conveyances and Assurances to be made of any Estate or Estates in Fee-simple, or for term of Life or Lives of any the premises, according to such Contracts as shall be agreed upon between the Purchaser or Purchasers, and the said Trustees, or any five or more of them respectively, shall be good and effectual in Law, to all intents and purposes: And all and every Purchaser and Purchasers of the premises, or any part thereof, his and their Heirs, Successors and Assigns respectively, shall have, hold and enjoy the

b premises that shall be by him or them so purchased, discharged of all Trusts and Accompts, whereunto the said Trustees, or any or either of them, are or may be lyable by vertue of this Act; and of all Suits and Questions that may arise, or be moved upon pretence of Sale at Under-values; and of all Claims and Demands whatsoever; and of all Incumbrances made by the said Trustees, or any claiming under them or any of them: And that the same shall not be lyable unto, but freed and discharged of and from all and all maner of Statutes, Judgements, Recognizances, Dowers, Joyntures, and other Acts and Incumbrances whatsoever, had, made, done or suffered, or to be had, made,

c done or suffered, by, from or under the said Trustees, or any of them respectively, other then such Conveyances and Assurances as shall be had, made, done or suffered, in performance and pursuance of the Sales and Contracts respectively made, according to the meaning of this present Act.

And if any Action shall be brought against the said Trustees, Treasurers, or other Officers or Officer, or any of them, in execution of this Act, or any former Act, Ordinance, Orders or Instructions whereunto it relates, That then he or they are hereby enabled to plead the General Issue, and to give this Act in Evidence: And if Judge-

d ment shall be had for the Defendant or Defendants in such Action, he and they shall recover double Costs.

And whereas the Parliament do finde it necessary to raise a considerable Sum of Money for the carrying on the Services of the Navy, Be it therefore Enacted, That the sum of Two hundred thousand pounds shall be borrowed upon the Security of the Lands of the said persons, whose Estates are by this Act appointed to be sold by way of Doubling, the like sum as it is or shall be due unto any person or persons, Body Politique or Corporate, upon the Publique Faith; or which might have been Doubled by vertue of any Act, Order or Ordinance of this present Parliament, and hath not formerly been Doubled upon the credit of Bishops, and Deans and Chapters Lands;

a or upon the Lands of the late King, Queen and Prince, or upon the Fee-Farm Rents: And that all and every person and persons, Body Politique or Corporate, for every sum or sums of Money he or they shall further lend, may and shall be secured the moneys formerly owing as aforesaid; And such other moneys as he or they shall advance for the raising of Two hundred thousand pounds, upon the Lands of the said persons in this Act named, in such sort as by the beforementioned Act, Entituled, *An Act for the Sale of several Lands and Estates forfeited to the Commonwealth for Treason*, is Enacted or Provided. And the said Trustees are hereby Impowered and *b* Authorized to pursue the Rules and Instructions for Doubling of money, as is appointed and declared in the several Acts of this present Parliament for the sale of Dean and Chapters Lands.

And be it further Enacted, That Sir John Wollaston Knight and Alderman of the City of London, Thomas Andrews, John Dethick and Francis Allein, Aldermen of the said City, shall be Treasurers for the said Service: and that they or any two of them, are hereby impowered and authorized to receive the said Two hundred thousand pounds, and all other such sum and sums of money as from time to time ought to be paid in to the Treasury by vertue of this Act, which *c* shall be issued out and paid according to such Orders, Warrants, Directions and Instructions, as they shall from time to time receive from the Parliament, for the use of the Navy as aforesaid.

And be it further Enacted by the Authority aforesaid, That the Register named in the said Act (Entituled, *An Act for the Sale of several Lands and Estates, forfeited to the Commonwealth for Treason*) [196] and his Deputy, are hereby authorized and required, upon a Warrant or Warrants from the said Trustees, to make out, rate and sign, one or more Particulars of all and every the premises hereby appointed to be sold: And that the respective Trustees do upon such Particular *d* proceed to Contract with any Purchaser or Purchasers for the same, and to make sale thereof accordingly.

And be it further Enacted and Ordained, That the respective Trustees, Treasurers, Register, Register-Accomptant, and Surveyor-General, named in the aforesaid *Act for sale of several Lands and Estates forfeited to the Commonwealth for Treason*, shall do, execute, observe and keep, all and every the like Powers, Authorities, Orders, Directions and Instructions, in relation to the premises hereby appointed to be sold, or any of them, as they and every of them ought to do, or to have done in reference to other the Manors, Lands, Tenements and Hereditaments of the said Traytors and persons in the said former Act mentioned; and shall have and receive such and the like Salaries and *a* Fees for them and their Clerks respectively, and in such sort and maner, as they and every of them respectively are and ought to have and receive for their respective Services and Imployments, touching the sale of other the Manors, Lands, Tenements and Hereditaments, by the aforesaid Act appointed to be sold.

Provided also, That if any person or persons shall Double any sum of money upon forged Debentures, or other false Certificates, or any other fraudulent way or means, and thereof shall be convicted by Oath before the Commissioners for Obstructions, within one year after such Doubling, every such person so offending shall forfeit treble the said *b* Sum, the one Moyety thereof to the use of the Commonwealth, and the other Moyety to such person or persons as shall discover the same before the said Commissioners for Obstructions in this Act named, and shall be committed to prison, and his Estate sequestred by the said Commissioners for Obstructions until payment thereof.

Provided always, and be it further Enacted, That all and every person or persons having any Estate, Right, Title or Interest, of, in or unto any the Lands, Tenements or Hereditaments by this Act intended or mentioned to be put to Sale, or that hath any Statute, Judgement, Recognizance or Rent which were without fraud, and for *c* good and valuable Consideration had, made and acknowledged before any Treason respectively committed by any of the persons in this Act named, whose Estates are appointed to be sold, and shall obtain an Allowance thereof by the said Commissioners for removing of Obstructions, before the First day of December, One thousand six hundred fifty and two, That then the same shall be good and effectual to such person or persons, their Executors, Administrators and Assigns respectively, to all intents and purposes, according to the Tenor thereof, Any thing in this Act to the contrary in any wise notwithstanding.

And be it further Enacted by this present Parliament, and by *d* Authority thereof, That all Reversions and Remainders expectant upon any Estate Tail, upon any Conveyance made by the said Traitor or Traitors, or any other person or persons, by or under whom they or any of them Claim, of any the Manors, Lands, Tenements or Hereditaments of any the Traitor or Traitors in this Act, or in the aforesaid *Act for Sale of several Lands and Estates forfeited to the Commonwealth for Treason*, named, not actually vested in the possession of such Tenant in Tail by the death of such Traytor or Traytors, before the Five and twentieth day of March, One thousand six hundred fifty two, which by Fine and Recovery might be docqued by any of the said Traytor or Traytors, are and shall be to all intents and purposes forfeited for their said Treasons; And as well the said Traytors and *a* their Heirs and Assigns, and all other persons and their heirs in Reversion or Remainder upon any such Estate, shall be for ever barred, as if such Traytor or Traytors had actually levied a Fine, and suffered a Recovery for doing thereof, any Allowance, Law, Statute or Usage to the contrary in any wise notwithstanding.

Provided always, and be it further Enacted, That the Trustees in this Act named, shall be, and are hereby Authorized and Required to Convey unto George Joyce of Portland, in the County of Dorset Esq; his Heirs and Assigns for ever, Lands, Tenements and Hereditaments appointed by this Act to be sold, of the clear Yearly value of One
b hundred pounds *per annum*, over and above all Charges and Reprizes, Any thing in this or any former Act contained to the contrary in any wise notwithstanding.

Provided also, That this Act nor any thing therein contained, shall not extend nor be prejudicial unto, bar or destroy, extinguish nor take away any Right, Interest, Reversion or Remainder saved or preserved, or mentioned or intended to be saved or preserved unto Charls Fleetwood Esq; and unto Frances his late wife, their or either of their Heirs or Assigns, unto any Manors, Lands, Tenements or Hereditaments whatsoever, mentioned in or by the late *Act for Sale of several* [197]
c Lands and Estates forfeited to the Commonwealth for Treason, by Order of Parliament published the Sixteenth day of July, One thousand six hundred fifty and one.

Provided nevertheless, and it is further Enacted, That in recompence and satisfaction of such Judgements, Statutes, Recognizances, Mortgages and other Incumbrances, as by the true intent and provision of this Act are to be satisfied, the said Trustees or any five or more of them, upon the return of the respective Surveys, are hereby Impowered and Authorized to set out such proportion of the Lands so surveyed, as will be sufficient to satisfie such Incumbrance and Incum-
d brances; And after such Incumbrances proved, and the Debts allowed of by the Commissioners for removing of Obstructions, to sell and convey such proportionable Part of the said Lands so surveyed, to such Creditor or Creditors or their Assigns, in recompence and satisfaction of such Incumbrance and Incumbrances, either for Life, Lives, Years or in Fee, the said Trustees taking care in satisfying such Incumbrances, to satisfie the same in such priority and course as the same ought to be satisfied by the Laws of this Land; and upon such Conveyance and Conveyances made, the said Creditor and Creditors, their Heirs, Executors, Administrators or Assigns, shall acknowledge Satisfaction upon Record, or otherwise release and discharge such Judgements, Statutes, Recognizances, Mortgages and other Incum-

a brances respectively, as the Council of the said Trustees and for the Commonwealth shall direct and advise: And such Acknowledgement, Release and Discharge shall be good and effectual in Law to discharge the said Debts and Incumbrances, as against the residue of the said Lands intended to be sold by this Act, Any Law, Statute or Usage to the contrary in any wise notwithstanding.

Passed 4 *August.*

1652. Cap. 23.

LANDS AND ESTATES OF SEVERAL OTHER PERSONS FORFEITED FOR TREASON, TO BE SOLD.

a   Whereas the Estates of John Gifford of Eastbury in the county of [210] Berks Gent. Stephen Frewen Doctor in Divinity, late of the University of Oxford, William Lord Powis, Joseph Jean of Liscard in the county of Cornwal Gent. Walter Langdon of Cavan in the same county Esq; George Collins of Helston in the same county, Nicholas Burlase of Treludda in the same county, Thomas Jack of St. Just in the same county, Richard Porter of Lanivels in the same county, William Spry of Blisland in the same county Gent. Degory Tremain of Pounstock in the same county Gent. William Knights of Brinton in the county of Huntingdon Clerk, Sir Thomas Aston late of Aston in

b the county of Chester Baronet, deceased; John Bretland of Thorncliff in the same county Gent. Edward Bostock of Harup in the same county Yeoman, John Barnet of Sound in the Parish of Wrenbury in the same county, Pierce Dod of Broxton in the same county Gent. Richard Egerton of Ridley in the same county, Francis Gamul of Chester Esqs; Richard Grantham of Halle in the county of Chester aforesaid Yeoman; Richard Green of Congleton in the same county, George Hope of Doddleston in the same county, Esqs; William Hutchins late of Gosworth in the same county Clerk, deceased; John Harper of Dutton in the same county, Husbandman, William Hardye

c of Hale in the same county Husbandman, Thomas Hodgkey of Burwardsley in the same county Husbandman, Urian Leighe of Adlington in the same county Gent. John Ruter late of Kingsley in the same county Gent. deceased, John Robinson sometime of Brereton in the same county Clerk, William Sharman of Oldstcastle in the same county, William Wilbraham late of Woodhaye in the same county Gent. deceased, Peter Worth of Titherington in the same county Gent. John Walker of Little Budworth in the same county Yeoman, Jeffry Whalley of Tatton in the same county Yeoman, Peter Wright of Lostock-Gralam in the same county, John Biddulph of Biddulph in the county of Stafford Esq; Robert Chantrel of Knoctorum cum Woodchurch in the county of Chester, Thomas Pool of Morley in the same county Gent. George Parsons of Beeston in the same county, yeoman, Edward Standish of Wooson in the county of Lancaster Esq; Thomas Weeksteed of Marberry in the county of Chester Gent. Rice Beamont

a of Egermon in the county of Cumberland yeoman, Thomas Lindsey of
Rickerby in the same county Gent. Simon Musgrave of Fairbank in
the same county Esq; sir William Musgrave of Fairbank in the same
county Knight, William Rain of Penreth in the same county yeoman,
Robert Storey of Ednol in the same county yeoman, Thomas Wibergh
of St. Bees in the same county Esq; Lancellot Walker of Thorpennow
in the same county Gent. Robert Whitfield of Randelholm in the same
county Gent. Lodowick West of Little Salkeld late one of the Prebends
of Carlisle, sir Charls Howard of Croglin in the same county Knight,
George Skelton of Witherel-Abby [Wetherall Priory] in the same county
b Gent. Andrew Huddleston of Hutton-John in the said county Esq; Pool
Turvile of Grazeley in the county of Derby, John Merry of Bressencoat
in the same county Esq; Richard Arundel of Walkampton in the county
of Devon Esq; Nicholson Bear of Silferton in the same county Gent.
Henry Bidlake of Bridstow in the same county, John Cox of Combe-
Pine in the same county yeoman, Richard Galhampton of Newton-
Ferris in the same county Gent. Robert Hill of Woodberry in the
same county Gent. John Jacob senior of Tavistock in the same county
Gent. Richard Lane of Mary-Church in the same county Gent. John
Little-John of Tavistock in the same county Gent. Thomas Lang of
c Plimpton in the same county Innkeeper, Richard Keyes of Holm alias
Holden in the same county Clerk, George Moor of Culhampton in the
same county Esq; Thomas Rich of Worthel in the same county Gent.
John Somaster of Stoakenham in the same county, Richard Trennick
of Ugborow in the same county yeoman, Thomas Wood of Orchard
in the same county Esquire, Robert Emerson of Ludwel in the county
of Durham Gent. Robert Ellis of Paulharburn in the county of York,
Ralph Gray of Trumblehill in the county of Durham yeoman, John
Hilton of Hilton in the same county Esq; Richard Harrison of Over-
frierside in the said county Gent. Katherine Conyers of   in
d the same county, sir John Morley of Newcastle upon Tine Knight, sir
John Mennes late of Winlaton in the county of Durham, Knight; sir [211]
John Sommerset of Gaynford in the same county, Kt. James Ascough
of Middleton on Rowe in the same county; Thomas Braithwait of
Neesam Abby in the county of York, Gent. Anthony Bulmer of Ketton
in the county of Durham, Esq; Cuthbert Collingwood of Dawden in
the same county, Esq; Ralph Coatsworth of Great Stainton in the
same county, Gent. John Errington of Rudby in the county of York,
Esquire; John Errington of Elton in the county of Durham, Gent.
Sir William Fenwick of Scrimarston in the same county, Knight,
William Hall of Greencroft in the same county, Gent. Ralph Millet of
Mayland in the same county, Gent. Michael Pudsey of Middleton-

a George in the same county, Gent. William Power of the City of Durham; Lancelot Salkeld late of Skirmingham in the same county, Gent. William Sherratton of Elwick in the same county; Lawrence Sawyer of Yarum in the county of York, Esquire; Thomas Wray of Beamish in the county of Durham, Esquire; Andrew Young of   in the county of York, Esquire, late called Sir Andrew Young, Knight; Henry Lord Arundel, Baron of Warder; Richard Burleton of Stalbridge in the county of Dorset, Linen-draper; John Coplestone late of Nash in the same county. William Gardner late of Weymouth in the said county of Dorset, Merchant; William Gayler of Whitchurch *b* in the same county, Yeoman; Thomas Jervis of   in the same county, Gent. Thomas Loup of Henbury in the Parish of Sturminster-Marshal in the said county of Dorset; Zachary Newberry of Stockland in the same county, Yeoman; Nicholas Pain of Causeway in Roddipol in the same county, Gent. Anthony Salter of the City of Exeter, Apothecary; John Samwaies late of Bradway in the county of Dorset, Gent. John Turnor of Woottonfitzpain in the same county, Husbandman; Alexander Kains of Raddipool in the same county, Gent. Thomas White of Fittleford in the same county, Gent. George White of Spettsberry in the same county;   Anderton of Althorn *c* in the county of Essex; Richard Fanshaw of Barking in the same county, Esquire; John Hills of Goldanger in the same county; Doctor Norton of Colchester in the same county;   Wenlock of Langham in the same county; James Clerk of Ilford in the same county; William Shelton alias Sheldon of Curringham in the same county, Esq; Thomas Wortham of Reckinden in the same county; Thomas Charnock of Lidney in the county of Gloucester, George Guise of Sandhurst in the same county; John Portlock late of Cirencester in the same county, deceased; Anthony Rolles of Pannington in the same county; Sir Bainham Throgmorton of Clowerwal in the *d* same county, Baronet; Thomas Coningsby late of North-Mims in the county of Hertford, Esquire, deceased; Henry Lord Morley and Mountoagle; Robert Shepheard sometime of Cliff Park in the county of Northampton; Millicent Prat of Cherryorton in the county of Huntington; Thomas Acton of Burton in the county of Worcester; Doctor Hugh Lloyd of St. Andrews in the county of Glamorgan; Henry Morgan of Stoak-Edy in the county of Hereford; Edward Slaughter of Bishops-frome in the same county; James Scudamore of Langarran in the same county; Evan Jones of Stockton in the same county; Rowland Scudamore of Treworgan in the same county; Robert Wigmore of Lucton in the same county, Gent. Edward Masters of Wilsborough in the county of Kent; Francis Nethersole

THIRD ACT, 1652.

a of Ash in the same county, Esquire; John Trout of Feversham in the same county; Ralph Clark of Frognal in the same county; William Allenson late of Woolton-magna in the county of Lancaster; William Arnold of Crosby in the same county; James Bradley of Bryning in the same county, Gentleman; Thomas Beesly of Layton and Boughton in the same county; John Bond of Inkling-Green in the same county; John Barker of Weetley in the same county; Thomas Barns of Goose-nargh cum Whittingham in the same county; Robert Craven of Billington in the same county; Joseph Carter of Furnes in the same county, John Denton of Widnes in the *b* same county; William Darwen of Wavertree in the same county; Henry Doughty of Thornley in the same county; John Greehalgh late of Bramblesholm in the said county, Esquire, deceased; William Green of Torisholm in the same county; Charls Gerrard of Halsal in the same county, Esquire; George Hornby of Standish in the same county; Gilbert Haughton of Brinscals in the same county; Thomas Kirkby of Upper Raweliff cum Turnaker in the same county; John Key of Walmersley in the same county; William Lewis of Torkesteth, Clerk, in the same county; Richard Leyland of Abraham in the same county; Ellis Leyland of Woston in the same county; William Lamb *c* of Turnham in the same county; Philip Martingdal of Blackrod in the same county; William Melling of Chorley in the same county; Edward Norris late of Hale in the same county, Gent. deceased; Christopher Nicholson of Tatham in the same county; Hugh Pilkington of Coppul in the same county; Edward Prescot of Standish in the same county; Thomas Perkinson of Chipping in the same county; Lawrence Park of Cuesdal in the same county; James Rigby of Coppul in the same county; George Robinson of Bretherton in the same county; William Ratcliff of Foxdenton in the same county, Esquire, deceased; Thomas Richardson of Outraweliff in the same *d* county; John Robinson of Oldlaund in the same county; Sir John Redman of Writon in the same county, Knight; Henry Snart late of Bretherton in the same county, deceased; Ralph Scot of Pemberton in the same county; Richard Salvage of Rufforth in the same county; Richard Sudel of Fishwick in the same county; James Stampard of [212] Warton in the same county; Peter Travers of Skilmersdale in the same county; Henry Wood of Widnes in the same county; John Wainwright of Latham in the same county; Ellis Wright of Croston in the same county; James Ward of Osbulstone in the same county; James Anderton of Birchley in Billing in the same county, Esquire; Hugh Anderton of Euxton in the same county, Gent. James Anderton of Clayton in the same county Esquire; William Anderton of Ander-

a ton in the same county, Esquire; Henry Ashton of Blackrod in the same county, Gent. Robert Bootle late of Thornton in the same county, deceased; William Blundel of Crosby-Parva in the same county, Esquire; Alexander Barker of Dalton in the same county; John Berry of Haughton in the same county, John Brown of Standish in the same county; John Bamber of Layton in the same county; Edward Butler of Outraweliff in the same county; Henry Butler of Goosenargh cum Whittingham in the same county, Gent. Thomas Birtwisle of Huncoat in the same county, Gent. Thomas Brockholes of Cheyley in the same county; Thomas Brockholes of Hayton in the same county; Thomas
b Bains of Sellet in the same county, Gent. John Bradshaw of Scale in the same county, Gent. William Butler of Mierscough in the same county; John Cliff of Eccleston in the same county; Richard Carter of Widnes in the same county; Richard Chorley of Chorley in the same county, Esq; Jervase Clifton of Salming-grange in the same county, Gent. Thomas Clark of Catteral in the same county; Richard Cottam of Dilworth in the same county; George Conwel of Watton in the same county; John Calvert of Cockerum in the same county, Gent. Robert Chorley of Yealand in the same county; Jordan Crosland of Furnes in the same county, Esq; Edward Denton of Ditton in the
c same county; Hugh Dobson of Legrum in the same county; Thomas Dalton late of Turnham in the said county, deceased; Richard Eltonhead of Eltonhead junior, in the same county; Richard Eyves of Bradley and Fishwick in the same county; Nicholas Fizakerley late of Fizakerley in the same county, Gent. deceased; Robert Fizakerley late of Walton in the same county, deceased; Robert Fowl of Billington in the same county; John Fletcher of Burscoe in the same county; James Green of Tilsley cum Astley in the same county; Edward Gore of Alker in the same county; John Gregson of Latham in the same county; James Gorsuch of Scaresbrick in the same county, Gent.
d Thomas Gellibrand of Chorley in the same county, Gent. Richard Green of Bowerhouse in the same county, Gent. William Gradel of Ulneswalton in the same county; Thomas Grimshaw of Clayton in same county; Robert Grimshaw of Clayton aforesaid in the same county; Nicholas Grimshaw of Clayton in the same county; William Gerrard of Ashton in the same county, Baronet; Ralph Howard of Sutton senior, in the same county; Edward Howard of Eccleston junior, in the same county; Thomas Harrison of Speak in the same county; William Hesketh late of Northmeals in the same county, Esq; deceased; John Haughton of Parkhall in the same county, Esquire; William Houghton of Grimzargh in the same county, Gent. Christopher Harris of Chipping in the same county, Gent. Christopher

a Jackson of Bold in the same county; George Janyon of Blackrod in the same county; John Knowls of Par in the same county; Richard Kellet late of Fishwick in the same county, deceased; John Lancaster of Reynel in the same county, Esquire; George Livesey late of Sutton in the same county, Gent. deceased; John Lineaker of Widnes in the same county; John Lathom of Hugton in the same county; John Lawrenson of Hugton aforesaid in the same county; William Lathom of Allerton in the same county, Gent. Richard Lathom of Allerton aforesaid in the same county, Esquire; Edward Lathom of the same in the same county, Gent. Henry Lovelady of Alker in the same *b* county; Richard Lucas of Haughton in the same county; Abraham Langton of Hindley in the same county; Thomas Langtree of Langtree in the same county, Esquire; Richard Lathom of Perbold in the same county, Esquire; William Laburn of Torisholm in the same county; William Manwaring of Windle in the same county, Gent. Edward Midgeal of Goosenargh in the same county; Roger Marsh of the same in the same county; William Moor late of Derby, Gent. deceased; Andrew Mercer of Derby; Edmund Mollineux of Ince-Blundel in the county of Lancaster; John Melling of the same; John Mollineux of the same, Gent. Richard Moss of Lathom in the same *c* county, Skinner; Henry Mossock of Bickerstaff in the same county, Gent. Richard Moss of Skelmersdale in the same county, Dyer; Henry Moss of the same; Thomas Morley of Wymington in the same county, Gent. Philip Norris of Fornby in the same county; Henry Nelson of Madesley in the same county; William Naylor of Croston in the same county; William Norris of Adlington in the same county; Thomas Nelson of Wrightington in the same county; William Norris of Blackrod in the same county; Andrew Newsham of Little-Plumpton in the same county; Richard North of Docker junior, in the same county; Nicholas Newsham of Little-Plumpton in the same county; Francis *d* Orton of Woodplumpton in the same county; James Pemberton of Whiston in the same county; John Parker late of Bradkirk in the same county, Gent. deceased; Robert Pleshington of Dimples in the same county, Gent. Thomas Parkinson of Clawton in the same county; Lawrence Parkinson of Goosenargh in the said county; William Parker of Woolfal in the same county, Gent. Thomas Parkinson of Graston-Leigh in the same county; Ralph Par of Altham in the same county; John Parker of Loveley in the same county, Gent. [213] Lawrence Parkinson of Swinshead in the same county; William Preston of Ellel in the same county; Giles Park of Furnes in the same county; Richard Quick of Woolton-magna in the same county; James Rice of Crosby-magna in the same county; Edward Rice of

a Crosby-parva in the same county; Thomas Pearson of Mierscough in the same county; Thomas Parker of Graston-Leigh in the same county; George Rigmaden of Latham in the same county; John Rigby of Standish in the same county; Ralph Rishton senior of Whiteash in the same county; Ralph Rishton junior, of the same; Edward Rishton of Michaelhaies in the same county; William Rishton of Ponthaulgh in the same county; John Roscoe of Dalton in Furnes in the same county; Michael Rutter of Croston in the same county; Richard Shuttleworth of Bedd' Gent. Henry Stannanaught of Fizakerley in the same county; John Serjeant late of Derby, deceased;
b George Standish late of Derby, Gent. deceased; William Speakman of Latham in the county of Lancaster; Peter Stanley of Bickerstaff in the same county; John Smith of Euxton in the same county; John Senhouse of Ecclestone in the same county, Esquire; Lawrence Standish of Standish in the same county; John Smith of Conow in the same county; Lawrence Sudel of Fulwood in the same county; Thomas Shepheard of Preston in the same county; Thomas Sowerbuts of Samlesbury in the same county; Robert Sherburn of Little-Mitton in the same county, Esquire; Robert Serjeant of Alcliff in the same county; Thomas Singleton of Dendron in Furnes in the same county;
c George Turner of Garston in the same county; John Tickle of Alker in the same county; John Tickle of Derby, Edward Tutlock of Kirby in the same county; Hugh Tootle of Whitkel in the same county; John Tootle of Chorley in the same county; Cuthbert Trelfal of Goosenargh in the same county; Richard Thornton of Fence in the same county; John Talbot of Dinkley in the same county, Esquire; Christopher Townley of Curre in the same county, Gent. Lawrence Stannanaught of Kirby in the same county; John Turvor of Tunstal in the same county; Wil. Trelfal of Warton in the same county; Andrew Thistleton of Mierscough in the same county; Wil. Thompson of Eccleston magna in the same county; Edward Tilsley of Ashley in the same county; Edward Unsworth of Windle in the same county; Richard Urmston of Leigh in the same county, Esq; George Wetherby of Whiston in the same county, Gent. Richard Wadmough of Sutton in the same county, Gent. Hugh Webster of Eccleston in the same county; Thomas Welsh of Awton in the same county, Gent. John Whittle of Wheelton in the same county; Thomas Woodcock of Brindle in the same county; Robert Waring of Chorley in the same county; Hugh Waterforth of Mawdesley in the same county; John Westby of Mowbrick in the same county, Esq; Francis Westby of Mierscough in the same county; Robert White of Kirkland in the same county, deceased; George Westby of Uprawcliff in the same

a county, Gent. John Wilkinson of Furnes in the same county; Ralph Atterton of Newbold in the county of Leicester; Samuel Clark of Kingsthorp in the county of Northampton;   Lloyd of the City of London; Walter Astley of Pascal in the county of Stafford, Esquire; William Brand of Horncastle in the county of Lincoln; Sir Francis Bodenham late of Roel in the county of Rutland; George Brailsford of Harlaxden in the county of Lincoln; Charls Bagshaw of Bourn in the same county; William Coney of Stoak in the same county, Esq; John Farr of Epworth in the same county, Yeoman; Thomas Wells of Horncastle in the same county, Gent. deceased; Sir
b Philip Constable of Middle-Rason in the same county; Marmaduke Doleman of Botsford in the same county, Gent. John Johnson of Willoughby in the same county, Gent. John Mounson [Monson] of Minting in the same county, Esquire; Thomas Nayler of the Bail in the same county, Gent. John Plumpton of Waterton in the same county, Esquire; Samuel Fawcet late of Broad-street in the City of London, Gunner, deceased; John Francis at the Wardrobe, London; Mr. Froster [Forster] of Brentford in the county of Middlesex; Joseph Jackman of Covent-garden in the same county; Gabriel Sedgwick servant to the late Lord Cottington; Timothy Wright of the City of Westminster,
c Gent. Thomas Jones of Lantrissent in the county of Monmouth, Yeoman; John Lewis of Lantrissent in the same county; William Morgan of Wrengochin in the same county; Nathanael Prichard of Abergavenny in the same county; John Morgan of Pentrebach in the same county, Gent. William Flyer of Llandilloportholi, William Jones of Hardwick, both of the same county; Anthony Morgan of Casebuchan in the same county; John Morgan formerly of Trostrey, now of Lanarth in the same county; Walter Norris of Llandillo-Grassenny in the same county; Thomas Stubs of Llanvitherrin in the same county; Lord Charls Somerset late of Ragland in the same county;
d James Scudamore of Penrose in the same county; Richard Anguish of Scarming in the County of Norfolk; Clippesby Bacon of Corpusty in the same county; William Mason of Slowley in the same county, Esquire; Thomas Pitcher of Whitsonset in the same county; Sir Robert Winde of Turrington in the same county; Edmund Mumford of Weerham in the same county, Gent. John Parris of Pudding-norton in the same county; Thomas Holder of South Wheatley in the county of Notingham, Gent. Marmaduke Moor of Ordsal in the same county, Minister; William Tirwhit [Tyrwhitt] late of Laneham in the same county; Will. Bawd of Walgrave in the same county, Esq; George Bartram of Elswick in the county of Northumberland; Thomas Clavering of Learchild in the same county; Sir John Clavering of Caleley in the [214]

a same county, Knight; Francis Carnaby of Cogston in the same county, John Fenwick of Crookden in the same county, Thomas Ogle of Darrashal in the same county, Ralph Read of Chirton in the same county, Gent. John Rodham of Little-Houghton in the same county, Gent. Musgrave Ridley of Nillemondswich in the same county, Thomas Winkle of Harnham in the same county, Gent. Edward Carlton of Hesleside in the same county, Esq; Robert Dent of Biker in the same county, Robert Cramlington of Newsham in the same county, Esq; Sir William Fenwick of Meldon in the same county, Knight; Robert Fenwick of Westmasin in the same county, Gent. Thomas
b Fenwick of Brestwick in the same county, Gent. William Fenwick of Blagden in the same county, Gent. Sir Charls Howard of Plenmeller in the same county, Thomas Rotherford of Rootchester in the same county, William Swinborn of Nafferton in the same county, Esquire; George Thirlwal of Rothbury in the same county, Gent. Sir Nicholas Thornton of Netherwitton in the same county; George Wray of Lemonden in the same county, Esquire; Sir Edward Widdrington of Cartington in the same county; Ralph Widdrington of Colwel in the same county, Gent. Thomas Waterton of Carraw in the same county, Gent. Henry Widdrington of Ritton in the same county, Gent.
c Henry Widdrington of Bootland in the same county, Gent. Sir Charls Blount late of Bisciter in the county of Oxon, deceased; Francis Mildmay of Ammersden in the same county, Esquire; Richard Edwards of Pentrewarn in the county of Salop; George Kinaston of Eastwick in the same county, Gent. Sir Walter Blount of Mawley in the same county, Knight; Henry Englefield of Detton in the same county; Robert Baker late of Minchead in the county of Somerset, Yeoman, deceased; John Brag of Crewkhern in the same county, Gent. William Chilcot of Milverton in the same county, Gent. Richard Chaffey of Stoak under Hambden in the same county, Yeoman;
d Samuel Chaffey of Mountague in the same county, Free-Mason; Edward Chaffey of Stoak under Hambden in the same county, Yeoman; James Dorchester of Puckington in the same county; Lawrence Drake of Isle Abbots in the same county, Gent. Edward Davis of Lamyet in the same county, Gent. Robert Ford of Crewkhern in the same county, Gent. Richard Gay of Lincomb in the same county, Gent. William Gowen of Horsington in the same county, Esquire; William Gaylerd of Thorn in the same county, Richard Godwin of Ilmister in the county of Somerset aforesaid, Yeoman; John Hodges of Eastquantonhead in the same county; Thomas Hopkins of Tintenhull in the same county; John Horsey of Compton-Dundon in the same county; Thomas Jervis of Bruton in the same

THIRD ACT, 1652.

a county; Nathanael Jones of Bridge-water in the same county, Gent. Hugh Jones of the same; James Moor of Willeton in the same county, Husbandman; Richard Newcourt of Sumerton in the same county; William Noss of Lambrick in the same county, Gent. Henry Pike of St. Decumans in the same county; William Pike of the same, Clothier; George Prater of Nunney in the same county; John Roberts of Bridgewater in the same county, Gent. John Walker of Netherstow in the same county; John Walcot of Milburn Port in the same county, Esquire; Richard Weech of Street in the same county, Gent. John Wills of Chisleborough in the same county, Husbandman; Humphrey
b Wear of Kingston in the same county, Clerk; Giles Pointz of Oldcleeve in the same county, Esquire; Henry Fowel of Abbots-An in the county of Southampton, Gent. Anthony Gosling of Moorsted in the same county, Clerk; Doctor   Laney of Peterfield in the same county; James Mallet of Portsmouth in the same county; John Pinchin of Shalden in the same county, Gent. John Unwin of Ennington in the same county; William Budding of Clinton in the same county, Husbandman; William Chamberlain of Nash in the same county, Gent. Thomas Chamberlain of Lindhurst in the same county, Gent. Anthony Hide of Woodhouse in the same county; James Link-
c horn of Bowyet in the same county; Miles Philipson of Throp in the same county; Swithen Wells of Eastly in the same county, Gent. Francis Collier of Stone in the county of Stafford, Gent. Dud Dudley of Greenlodge in the same county; William Ellis of Coaton in the same county; John Gifford of Marston in the same county, Gent. Sir Edward Littleton of Pillington in the same county, Baronet, Timothy Starting of Uttoxeter in the same county; Humphrey Vize of Standon in the same county, Gent. Thomas Wooldridge of Acton in the same county, Husbandman; Walter Gifford of Hyon in the same county, Gent. John Gifford of Wolverhampton in the same county, Gent.
d Anthony Pomfret of Eshur in the county of Surrey; Christopher Wheeler of Hern in the same county; Henry Bellingham late of Newtimber deceased, in the county of Sussex; John Rigate of Hastings in the same county; William Gage late of Bentley in the same county; Anthony Rigby of Tillington in the same county; Thomas Allen of Laystuff in the county of Suffolk, Mariner; Anthony Mowsey of Cattam in the same county, deceased; Henry Thynne of Biddeston in the county of Wilts; Francis Toop of Knoyl in the same county; Miles Philipson of Tisbury in the same county; Edmund Wells of Littletondrew; Edward Barret of Droitwich junior in the county of Worcester; Edward Barret of the same, late called Sir Edward Barret; Colonel Dud Dudley of Dudley of the same county;

a Charls Kingston of Nanton-Beauchamp in the same county; Sir Edward Littleton of Little-Shelsey in the same county; Thomas Warmstree of   in the same county, Clerk; Thomas Acton of Bourton [215] in the same county, Esquire; Walter Blount of Soddington in the same county, Esquire; Thomas Chauncey of Kittermister [Kidderminster] in the same county; Major Frederick Winsor of Clains in the same county; Anthony Garnet of Kendal in the county of Westmerland, gent. Christopher Gilpin of Kentmire in the same county, gent. John Jackson of Shap in the same county, Yeoman; John Philipson of Hollinghow in the same county, gent. John Parker of Kendal in the
b same county, Yeoman; Robert Pattison of Sowerby in the same county; John Richardson of Crosby-Ravenswich in the same county, Yeoman; Henry Salkeld of Winton in the same county, Yeoman; Thomas Waller of Ewbank in the same county, Yeoman; William Fleming of Riddal in the same county, Esq; John Smith of Whitwal in the same county, Yeoman; Doctor   Ambrose late of Sheepley in the county of York, deceased; Thomas Awstwick of Pomfret in the same county; George Acklam of Bewholm in the same county, gent. Adam Bland second son of Sir Thomas Bland of Skippar in the same county; Thomas Brockhouse of Grimlington in the same county;
c George Beesley of Twisleton in the same county, gent. Richard Bowes of York, Mercer; John Chapman of Hurwoodale in the county of York; Sidney Constable of Sherburn in the same county, gent. Doctor Richard Chambers of   in the same county; Stephen Carre late of Sandisk in the same county, Yeoman; Major Lewis Carre of Lowkellerbey in the same county; Henry Cholmley of Tunstal in the same county; Thomas Danby late of Carre in the same county; William Doleman late of Duncoats in the same county, deceased; Robert Ellis of Towthorp in the same county, deceased; William Flintoft of Scarborough in the same county; John Fleming of
d in the county of Cumberland; Robert Freer of Newbridge in Netherdale in the county of York, deceased; Gabriel Freeman of Thirsk in the same county, Draper; William Frankland of Woodhall in the same county; Marmaduke Frank of Kneeton; William Goodman of Bramham alias Bramwich in the same county; Edward Hardcastle of Biggin in the same county, gent. George Hemsworth of Roche in the same county; John Howden of Grimlington in the same county, yeoman; Richard Hunter of Frodingham in the same county; Thomas Hardwick of Shadwel in the same county, Yeoman; Thomas Hitchin of Normanton in the same county; George Jackson late of York, Draper; Christopher Kidds of West-witton in the county of York aforesaid; Arthur Langfield of Seacroft in the same county; John

a Morley late of Whorlton, deceased, in the same county; Henry Marshal late of Foulforth in the same county, gent. Thomas Morley of Burton in the same county, gent. John Marsh late of Hallifax Doctor in Divinity, in the same county; Miles Newton of Littlethorp in the same county; Charls North of Whitguift in the same county; George Noudike of Wellam in the same county; John Parker of Raddampark in the same county; John Plumpton of Uslet in the same county, Esq; eldest son to Sir Edward Plumpton; John Pullen of Bishop-Mouncton in the same county; Fairfax Ringrose of Amotherby in the same county, gent. Sir John Redman late of Newcastle in the
b same county; Thomas Stanley of Bishopton in the same county, gent. John Smith of Awdfield in the same county, yeoman; Sir William Theakston late of   deceased; Edmund Tatham of Burton in the county of York, gent. John Tailer of London; Richard Vincent of Great-Smeaton in the said county of York; Stephen Whitwel of Cropton in the same county; Anthony Wharton of Eppleby in the same county; William Winsor of Fockerby in the same county; Darcy Washington of Hampsal in the same county; James Washington of the same in the same county; Christopher Anderton of Anderton in the same county, Esquire; Allen Ascough of Skewsby in the same
c county, Esq; Thomas Berney of Dolebank in the same county, gent. John Adamson of Thornton in the same county, yeoman; James Ascough of Dinsdale in the same county, gent. Dame   Armitage of Herthead in the same county; Henry Berney of Haddockstone in the same county, gent; Edward Barton of Towthorp in the same county; Thomas Bains of Twisleton in the same county; Mrs. Butler of Grisby in the same county; William Brigham of Witton in the same county; William Bulmer of Marrick in the same county, Esq; William Barber of Clint in the same county, yeoman; John Cansfield sometime called Sir John Cansfield of   in the same
d county; John Clifton of Worsal in the same county, yeoman; William Constable of Kathorp in the same county, Esquire; Matthew Constable of Benningholm-grange in the same county, gent. Marmaduke Cholmley of Bransby in the same county, Esq; John Constable of Kirbyknowl in the same county; Fairley Coulson of Libberston in the same county, yeoman; George Cockson of Bankhouse in the same county, gent. Philip Doleman of   in the same county, gent. Marmaduke Doleman of Middleton in the same county, gent. Thomas Doleman late of Duncoats in the same county, gent. deceased; John Danby of Leak in the same county; Edmund Danby of Burrowby in the same county; Thomas Empson of Goul in the same county; William late Lord Ewre the Grandfather, deceased; William Green

a of Lamoth in the same county; Robert Gale of Akeham-grange in the same county; William Hogg of Harrowgate in the same county, yeoman; Philip Hamerton of Purston in the same county; John Hebden of Clint in the same county; Marmaduke Holtby of Scakleton-grange in the same county; Peter Hawkins of Carperby in the same county, yeoman; John Knavesborough of Ferringsby in the same [216] county; Mrs.   Killingbeck of Killinghall Widow, in the same county; George Daniel of Thorp Brantington in the same county; Richard Lowther of Engleton in the same county, Esquire; Richard Longley of Millington in the same county, Esquire; John Middleton *b* late called Sir John Middleton of   in the same county; Mrs.   Waterton of   in the same county; Nicholas Morley of Standerber in the same county, Yeoman; Michael Metcalf of Little-Ottrington in the same county, Gent. John Mallory of Felton in the county of Northumberland; John Percy of Stubswalden in the county of York aforesaid; Sir George Palms of Naburn in the same county; Margaret Robinson now married to Thomas Metcalf of Ottrington in the same county; John Rider of Scarcroft in the same county; James Robinson of York; Lawrence Sayer of Worsal in the same county; Thomas Smith of Egton in the same county; James Singleton of *c* Marlington in the same county, Gent. deceased; William Stephenson of Thornton in the same county; Robert Trapps of Nidd in the same county, Esquire; Stephen Tempest late of Roundhay in the same county, Esquire, Thomas Tankard of Butterset in the same county; Charls Thimbleby of Carlton in the same county; John Vavasour of Willatoft in the same county, Gent. Andrew Young late called Sir Andrew Young of   in the county of York aforesaid; Bodenham Gunter of Gwenthor in the county of Brecon'; John Wintour of Lanvihangel in the same county; Doctor William Roberts of Llanliddon in the county of Denbigh; Edward Fox of Rheteskin in the *d* county of Mountgomery, Gent; Doctor William Lewis of Llanwyvy in the county of Merioneth; John Morgan of Trawsby-mill in the same county, Gent. Richard Dutton of Kefennern in the county of Flint; Tristram Lloyd of   in the same county; Mr.   Smith of   late servant to the Earl of Derby; Herbert Price of the Town of Brecon'; John Vaughan of   in the county of Radnor; Thomas Bennet of   in the county of Chester; John Tirer of   in the county of Salop; Andrew Richards of   in the county of Somerset; Parris Smith of   Thomas Earl of Berks; Sir Thomas Chamberlain of Oxon', Baronet; Thomas Webb son to Roger Webb of   in the county of Suffolk; Sir Richard Titchburn of   in the county of   Knight and Baronet, de-

THIRD ACT, 1652.   51

a ceased ; Sir Edward Plumpton of   in the county of
  Sir John Thimbleby of   in the county of Lincoln ; William
  Brand of   in the same county ; Henry Fernes late of Walders-
  wick in the county of Suffolk ; Richard Witherow of White-chappel
  in the county of   Mariner ; Littleton Clent of Knightwick in
  the county of Worcester ; Sir William Quadring of   in the
  county of Lincoln ; Norris Fines of   in the county of
  Henry Bidlake of Briddestow in the county of Devon ; Philip Philcot
  of the Grange in the county of Kent ; George Bag of   in the
  county of Devon, Esq ; Peter Hatton of   in the county of
b Chester ; Francis Giles of   in the county of Devon, Gent. John
  Arundel of Sithney in the county of Cornwal ; John Portlock late of
  Cirencester in the county of Glocester, deceased ; Pierce Mannaton of
  Stoak-Cliveland in the county of Cornwal ; Sir Thomas Dacre of Lever-
  cust [Lanercost] in the county of Cumberland, Knight ; and Thomas
  Brockholes of Heaton in the county of Lancaster ; Have been, and are
  hereby Declared and Adjudged to be justly Forfeited by them for
  their several Treasons against the Parliament and People of England.

  Be it therefore Enacted by this present Parliament, and the Authority
  thereof, That all the Manors, Lands, Tenements and Hereditaments
c which they the said John Gifford, Stephen Frewen, William Lord
  Powis, Joseph Jean, Walter Langdon, George Collins, Nicholas Bur-
  lase, Thomas Jack, Richard Porter, William Spry, Degory Tremain,
  William Knights, Sir Thomas Aston, John Bretland, Edward Bostock,
  John Barnet, Pierce Dod, Richard Egerton, Francis Gamul, Richard
  Grantham, Richard Green, George Hope, William Hutchins, John
  Harper, William Hardy, Thomas Hodgkey, Urian Leigh, John Rutter,
  John Robinson, William Sharman, William Wilbraham, Peter Worth,
  John Walker, Jeffry Whalley, Peter Wright, John Biddulph, Robert
  Chantrel, Thomas Pool, George Parsons, Edward Standish, Thomas
d Wicksted, Rice Beamount, Thomas Lindsey, Simon Musgrave, Sir
  William Musgrave, William Rain, Robert Storey, Thomas Wibergh,
  Lancelot Walker, Robert Whitfield, Lodowick West, Sir Charls
  Howard, George Skelton, Andrew Huddleston, Pool Turvile, John
  Merry, Richard Arundel, Nicholas Bear, Henry Bidlake, John Cox,
  Richard Galhampton, Robert Hill, John Jacob senior, Richard Lane,
  John Little-John, Thomas Lang, Richard Keyes, George Moor, Thomas
  Rich, John Somaster, Richard Trennick, Thomas Wood, Robert Emer-
  son, Robert Ellis, Ralph Gray, John Hilton, Richard Harrison,
  Katherine Conyers, Sir John Morley, Sir John Mennes, Sir John
  Somerset, James Ascough, Thomas Braithwait, Anthony Bulmer,
  Cuthbert Collingwood, Ralph Coatsworth, John Errington, John

a Errington, Sir William Fenwick, William Hall, Ralph Millet, Michael
Pudsey, William Power, Lancelot Salkeld, William Sharratton, Law-
rence Sayer, Thomas Wray, Andrew Young, Henry Lord Arundel,
Richard Burlton, John Coplestone, William Gardner, William Gayler,
Thomas Jervis, Thomas Loup, Zachary Newberry, Nicholas Pain,
Anthony Salter, John Samwaies, John Turner, Alexander Kains,
Thomas White, George White, Anderton, Richard Fanshaw,
John Hills, Doctor Norton, Wenlock, James Clark, William
Shelton alias Sheldon, Thomas Wortham, Thomas Charnock, George
Guise, John Portlock, Anthony Rolles, Sir Bainham Throgmorton,
b Thomas Coningsby, Henry Lord Morley and Mounteagle, Robert [217]
Shepheard, Millicent Prat, Thomas Acton, Hugh Lloyd, Henry
Morgan, Edward Slaughter, James Scudamore, Evan Jones, Rowland
Scudamore, Robert Wigmore, Edward Masters, Francis Nethersole,
John Trout, Ralph Clark, William Allenson, William Arnold, James
Bradley, Thomas Beesley, John Bond, John Barker, Thomas Barns,
Robert Craven, Joseph Carter, John Denton, William Darwyn, Henry
Doughty, John Greehalgh, William Green, Charls Gerrard, George
Hornby, Gilbert Houghton, Thomas Kirby, John Key, William Lewis,
Richard Leyland, Ellis Leyland, William Lamb, Philip Martingdal,
c William Melling, Edward Norris, Christopher Nicholson, Hugh Pilk-
ington, Edward Prescot, Thomas Perkinson, Lawrence Park, James
Rigby, George Robinson, William Ratcliff, Thomas Richardson, John
Robinson, Sir John Redman, Henry Snart, Ralph Scot, Richard
Salvage, Richard Sudel, James Stampard, Peter Travers, Henry Wood,
John Wainwright, Ellis Wright, James Ward, James Anderton, Hugh
Anderton, James Anderton, William Anderton, Henry Ashton, Robert
Bootle, William Blundel, Alexander Barker, John Berry, John Brown,
John Bamber, Edward Butler, Henry Butler, Thomas Birthwisle,
Thomas Brockholes, Thomas Brockholes, Thomas Bains, John Brad-
d shaw, William Butler, John Cliff, Richard Carter, Richard Chorley,
Jervase Clifton, Thomas Clerk, Richard Cottam, George Conwel, John
Calvert, Robert Chorley, Sir Jordan Crosland, Edward Denton, Hugh
Dobson, Thomas Dalton, Richard Eltonhead, Richard Eyves, Nicholas
Fizakerley, Robert Fizakerley, Robert Fowl, John Fletcher, James
Green, Edward Gore, John Grigson, James Gorsuch, Thomas Gelli-
brand, Richard Green, William Gradel, Thomas Grimshaw, Robert
Grimshaw, Nicholas Grimshaw, William Gerrard, Ralph Howard,
Edward Howard, Thomas Harrison, William Hesketh, John Haughton,
William Haughton, Christopher Harris, Christopher Jackson, George
Janyon, John Knowls, Richard Kellet, John Lancaster, George Livesey,
John Lineaker, John Lathom, John Lawrenson, William Lathom,

THIRD ACT, 1652. 53

a Richard Lathom, Edward Lathom, Henry Lovelady, Richard Lucas, Abraham Langton, Thomas Langtree, Richard Latham, William Laburn, William Manwaring, Edward Midgeal, Roger Marsh, William Moor, Andrew Mercer, Edmund Mollineux, John Melling, John Mollineux, Richard Moss, Henry Mossock, Richard Moss, Henry Moss, Thomas Morley, Philip Norris, Henry Nelson, William Naylor, William Norris, Thomas Nelson, William Norris, Andrew Newsham, Richard North, Nicholas Newsham, Francis Orton, **James Pemberton, John Parker,** Robert Pleshington, Thomas Parkinson, Lawrence Parkinson, William Parker, Thomas Parkinson, Ralph Par, John
b Parker, Lawrence Parkinson, William Preston, Giles Park, Richard Quick, James Rice, Edward Rice, Thomas Pearson, Thomas Parker, George Rigmaden, John Rigby, Ralph Rishton senior; Ralph Rishton junior; Edward Rishton, William Rishton, John Rosco, Michael Rutter, Richard **Shuttleworth,** Henry Stannanaught, **John Serjeant,** George Standish, **William** Speakman, Peter Stanley, John Smith, John Senhouse, Lawrence Standish, John Smith, Lawrence Sudel, Thomas Shepheard, Thomas Sowerbuts, Robert Sherburn, Robert Serjeant, Thomas Singleton, George Turner, John Tickle, John Tickle, Edward Tutlock, Hugh Tootle, John Tootle, Cuthbert Trelfal, Richard
c Thornton, John Talbot, Christopher Townley, Lawrence Stannanaught, John Turver, William Trelfal, **Andrew Thistleton,** William Thompson, Edward Tilsley, Edward Unsworth, Richard Urmston, George Wetherby, Richard **Wadmough,** Hugh **Webster,** Thomas Welsh, John Whittle, Thomas Woodcock, Robert Waring, Hugh Waterforth, John Westby, Francis Westby, Robert White, George Westby, John Wilkinson, Ralph Atterton, Samuel Clark,   Lloyd, Walter Astley, William Brand, Sir Francis Bodenham, George Brailsford, Charls Bagshaw, William Coney, John Far, Thomas Wells, Sir Philip Constable, Marmaduke Doleman, John Johnson, John Mounson, Thomas
d Nayler, John Plumpton, Samuel Fawcet, John Francis,   Forster, Joseph Jackman, Gabriel Sedgwick, Timothy Wright, Thomas Jones, John Lewis, William Morgan, Nathanael Prichard, John Morgan, William **Flyer, William Jones,** Anthony Morgan, John Morgan, Walter Norris, Thomas Stubs, Lord Charls Somerset, James Scudamore, Richard Anguish, Clippesby Bacon, William Mason, **Thomas Pitcher,** Sir Robert Winde, Edmund **Mumford,** John Parris, **Thomas Holder,** Marmaduke Moor, William **Tirwhit,** William Bawd, **George Bartram,** Thomas Clavering, Sir John Clavering, Francis Carnaby, John Fenwick, Thomas Ogle, Ralph Read, **John** Roddam, Musgrave Ridley, Thomas Winkle, Edward Carlton, **Robert Dent,** Robert Cramlington, Sir **William Fenwick,** Robert **Fenwick,** Thomas Fenwick, William Fen-

a wick, Sir Charls Howard, Thomas Rotherford, William Swinborn, George Thirlwal, Sir Nicholas Thornton, George Wray, Sir Edward Widdrington, Ralph Widdrington, Thomas Waterton, Henry Widdrington, Henry Widdrington, Sir Charls Blount, Francis Mildmay, Richard Edwards, George Kinaston, Sir Walter Blount, Henry Englefield, Robert Baker, John Brag, William Chilcot, Richard Chaffey, Samuel Chaffey, Edward Chaffey, James Dorchester, Lawrence Drake, Edward Davis, Robert Ford, Richard Gay, William Gowen, William Gaylerd, Richard Godwyn, John Hodges, Thomas Hopkins, John Horsey, Thomas Jervis, Nathanael Jones, Hugh Jones,
b James Moor, Richard Newcourt, William Noss, Henry Pike, William Pike, George Prater, John Roberts, John Walker, John Walcot, Richard Weech, John Wills, Humphrey Wear, Giles Pointz, Henry Fowel, Anthony Gosling, Doctor   Laney, James Mallet, John [218] Pinchin, John Unwyn, William Budding, William Chamberlain, Thomas Chamberlain, Anthony Hide, James Linkhorn, Miles Philipson, Swithen Wells, Francis Collier, Dud Dudley, William Ellis, John Gifford, Sir Edward Littleton, Timothy Starting, Humphrey Vize, Thomas Wooldridge, Walter Gifford, John Gifford, Anthony Pomfret, Christopher Wheeler, Henry Bellingham, John Rigate, William Gage,
c Anthony Rigby, Thomas Allen, Anthony Mowsey, Henry Thynne, Francis Toop, Miles Philipson, Edmund Wells, Edward Barret, Edward Barret, Colonel Dud Dudley, Charls Kingston, Sir Edward Littleton, Thomas Warmstree, Thomas Acton, Walter Blount, Tho. Chauncey, Maj. Fredrick Winsor, Anthony Garnet, Christopher Gilpin, John Jackson, John Philipson, John Parker, Robert Pattison, John Richardson, Henry Salkeld, Thomas Waller, William Fleming, John Smith, Doctor   Ambrose, Thomas Awstwick, George Acklam, Adam Bland, Thomas Brockhouse, George Beesley, Richard Bowes, John Chapman, Sidney Constable, Doctor
d Richard Chambers, Stephen Carre, Major Lewis Carre, Henry Cholmley, Thomas Danby, William Doleman, Robert Ellis, William Flintoft, John Fleming, Robert Freer, Gabriel Freeman, William Frankland, Marmaduke Frank, William Goodman, Edward Hardcastle, George Hemsworth, John Howden, Richard Hunter, Thomas Hardwick, Thomas Hitchin, George Jackson, Christopher Kidds, Arthur Langfield, John Morley, Henry Marshal, Thomas Morley, John Marsh, Miles Newton, Charls North, George Noudike, John Parker, John Plumpton, John Pullen, Fairfax Ringrose, Sir John Redman, Thomas Stanley, John Smith, Sir William Theakston, Edmund Tatham, John Taylor, Richard Vincent, Stephen Whitwel, Anthony Wharton, William Winsor, Darcy Washington, James Washington, Christopher

THIRD ACT, 1652. 55

a Anderton, Allen Ascough, Thomas Berney, John Adamson, James
Ascough, Dame   Armitage, Henry Berney, Edward Barton,
Thomas Bains, Mrs.   Butler, William Brigham, William
Bulmer, William Barber, John Cansfield, John Clifton, William Constable, Matthew Constable, Marmaduke Cholmley, John Constable, Fairley Coulson, George Cockson, Philip Doleman, Marmaduke Doleman, Thomas Doleman, John Danby, Edmund Danby, Thomas Empson, William late Lord Ewre, William Green, Robert Gale, William Hogg, Philip Hamerton, John Hebden, Marmaduke Holtby, Peter Hawkins, John Knavesborough, Mrs.   Killingbeck, George Daniel, Richard
b Lowther, Richard Langley, John Middleton, Mrs.   Waterton, Nicholas Morley, Michael Metcalf, John Mallory, John Percy, Sir George Palms, Margaret Robinson, John Rider, James Robinson, Lawrence Sayer, Thomas Smith, James Singleton, William Stephenson, Robert Trapps, Stephen Tempest, Thomas Tankard, Charls Thimbleby, John Vavasour, Andrew Young, Bodenham Gunter, John Wintour, Doctor William Roberts, Edward Fox, Doctor William Lewis, John Morgan, Richard Dutton, Tristram Lloyd,   Smith, Herbert Price, John Vaughan, Thomas Bennet, John Tirer, Andrew Richards, Parris Smith, Thomas Earl of Berks, Sir Thomas Chamberlain, Thomas
c Webb, Sir Richard Titchburn, Sir Edward Plumpton, Sir John Thimbleby, William Brand, Henry Fernes, Richard Witherow, Littleton Clent, Sir William Quadring, Norris Fines, Henry Bidlake, Philip Philcot, George Bag, Peter Hatton, Francis Giles, John Arundel, John Portlock, Pierce Mannaton, Sir Thomas Dacre and Thomas Brockholes, or any of them, or any for their Use or Uses, or in trust for any of them were seized or possessed of in Possession, Reversion or Remainder, on the Twentieth day of May, One thousand six hundred, forty two, or at any time since; And all Rights of Entry, and the whole Estates, Rights, Tithes and Interests of them and every
d of them, in or to the said Manors, Lands, Tenements or Hereditaments which they or any of them had the said Twentieth day of May, One thousand six hundred forty two, or at any time since (excepting Rectories Impropriate, Tithes, Composition for Tithes, Portions of Tithes, Donatives Oblations, Obventions and Rents issuing out of Tithes) Be and are hereby vested, adjudged and deemed to be, and are hereby in the Real and Actual Possession and Seisin of William Skinner, William Robinson, Matthias Valentine, Samuel Gooking, Henry Sealy, William Lisle and Arthur Samuel, and the Survivors and Survivor of them and their Heirs and Assigns; And that they and the Survivors and Survivor of them and their Heirs, shall and may have the Benefit and Advantage of the said Rights of Entry unto

a the said Manors, Lands, Tenements and Hereditaments, and every of them; And that they, their Heirs and Assigns shall hold all and every part and parcel of the said Manors and premises, as of the Manor of East Greenwich in Free Socage, by Fealty onely, and by no other Tenure or Service whatsoever. Nevertheless, upon trust and confidence, that the said William Skinner, and other the persons aforenamed, or any Five or more of them, shall have, hold and enjoy all and singular the premises, and every of them, subject to such Trust and Uses as by this Act, or in or by Authority of Parliament shall be hereafter directed and appointed; Saving to all and every person and *b* persons, Bodies Politique and Corporate, their Heirs, Successors, Executors, Administrators and Assigns, and every of them, other then the said John Gifford, Stephen **Frewen, William Lord Powis,** Joseph Jean, Walter Langdon, George Collins, Nicholas Burlase, Thomas Jack, Richard Porter, William Spry, Degory Tremain, William Knights, Sir Thomas Aston, John Bretland, Edward Bostock, John Barnet, Pierce Dod, Richard Egerton, Francis Gamul, Richard Grantham, Richard Green, George Hope, William Hutchins, John Harper, William Hardy, Thomas Hodgkey, Urian Leigh, John Rutter, John Robinson, William Sharman, William Wilbraham, Peter Worth, John [219] *c* Walker, Jeffry Whalley, Peter Wright, John Biddulph, Robert Chantrel, Thomas Pool, George Parsons, Edward Standish, Thomas Wicksted, Rice Beamount, Thomas Lindsey, Simon Musgrave, Sir William Musgrave, William Rain, Robert Storey, Thomas Wibergh, Lancelot Walker, Robert Whitfield, Lodowick West, Sir Charles Howard, George Skelton, Andrew Huddleston, Pool Turvile, John Merry, Richard Arundel, Nicholas Bear, Henry Bidlake, John Cox, Richard Galhampton, Robert Hill, John Jacob senior, Richard Lane, John Little-John, Thomas Lang, Richard Keyes, George Moor, Thomas Rich, John Somaster, Richard Trennick, Thomas Wood, Robert *d* Emerson, Robert Ellis, Ralph Gray, John Hilton, Richard Harrison, Katherine Conyers, Sir John Morley, Sir John Mennes, Sir John Somerset, James Ascough, Thomas Braithwait, Anthony Bulmer, Cuthbert Collingwood, Ralph Coatsworth, John Errington, John Errington, Sir William Fenwick, William Hall, Ralph Millet, Michael Pudsey, William Power, Lancelot Salkeld, William Sharratton. Lawrence Sayer, Thomas Wray, Andrew Young, Henry Lord Arundel, Richard Burlton, John Coplestone, William Gardner, William Gayler, Thomas Jervis, Thomas Loup, Zachary Newberry, Nicholas Pain, Anthony Salter, John Samwaies, John Turner, Alexander Kains, Thomas White, George White,   Anderton, Richard Fanshaw, John Hills, Doctor Norton,   Wenlock, James Clark, William

THIRD ACT, 1652.

a Shelton alias Sheldon, Thomas Wortham, Thomas Charnock, George Guise, John Portlock, Anthony Rolles, Sir Bainham Throgmorton, Thomas Coningsby, Henry Lord Morley and Mounteagle, Robert Shepheard, Millicent Prat, Thomas Acton, Hugh Lloyd, Henry Morgan, Edward Slaughter, James Scudamore, Evan Jones, Rowland Scudamore, Robert Wigmore, Edward Masters, Francis Nethersole, John Trout, Ralph Clark, William Allenson, William Arnold, James Bradley, Thomas Beesley, John Bond, John Barker, Thomas Barns, Robert Craven, Joseph Carter, John Denton, William Darwyn, Henry Doughty, John Greehalgh, William Green, Charls Gerrard, George

b Hornby, Gilbert Houghton, Thomas Kirby, John Key, William Lewis, Richard Leyland, Ellis Leyland, William Lamb, Philip Martingdal, William Melling, Edward Norris, Christopher Nicholson, Hugh Pilkington, Edward Prescot, Thomas Perkinson, Lawrence Park, James Rigby, George Robinson, William Ratcliff, Thomas Richardson, John Robinson, Sir John Redman, Henry Snart, Ralph Scot, Richard Salvage, Richard Sudel, James Stampard, Peter Travers, Henry Wood, John Wainwright, Ellis Wright, James Ward, James Anderton, Hugh Anderton, James Anderton, William Anderton, Henry Ashton, Robert Bootle, William Blundel, Alexander Barker, John Berry, John Brown,

c John Bamber, Edward Butler, Henry Butler, Thomas Birthwisle, Thomas Brockholes, Thomas Brockholes, Thomas Bains, John Bradshaw, William Butler, John Cliff, Richard Carter, Richard Chorley, Jervase Clifton, Thomas Clerk, Richard Cottam, George Conwel, John Calvert, Robert Chorley, Sir Jordan Crosland, Edward Denton, Hugh Dobson, Thomas Dalton, Richard Eltonhead, Richard Eyves, Nicholas Fizakerley, Robert Fizakerley, Robert Fowl, John Fletcher, James Green, Edward Gore, John Grigson, James Gorsuch, Thomas Gellibrand, Richard Green, William Gradel, Thomas Grimshaw, Robert Grimshaw, Nicholas Grimshaw, William Gerrard, Ralph Howard,

d Edward Howard, Thomas Harrison, William Hesketh, John Haughton, William Haughton, Christopher Harris, Christopher Jackson, George Janyon, John Knowls, Richard Kellet, John Lancaster, George Livesey, John Lineaker, John Lathom, John Lawrenson, William Lathom, Richard Lathom, Edward Lathom, Henry Lovelady, Richard Lucas, Abraham Langton, Thomas Langtree, Richard Latham, William Laburn, William Manwaring, Edward Midgeal, Roger Marsh, William Moor, Andrew Mercer, Edmund Mollineux, John Melling, John Mollineux, Richard Moss, Henry Moss,[1] Richard Moss, Henry Moss, Thomas Morley, Philip Norris, Henry Nelson, William Naylor, William

---

[1] Mossock on pp. 43*c*, 53*a*.

58   ROYALIST CONFISCATION ACTS.

a Norris, Thomas Nelson, William Norris, Andrew Newsham, Richard North, Nicholas Newsham, Francis Orton, James Pemberton, John Parker, Robert Pleshington, Thomas Parkinson, Lawrence Parkinson, William Parker, Thomas Parkinson, Ralph Par, John Parker, Lawrence Parkinson, William Preston, Giles Park, Richard Quick, James Rice, Edward Rice, Thomas Pearson, Thomas Parker, George Rigmaden, John Rigby, Ralph Rishton, senior; Ralph Rishton, junior; Edward Rishton, William Rishton, John Rosco, Michael Rutter, Richard Shuttleworth, Henry Stannanaught, John Serjeant, George Standish, William Speakman, Peter Stanley, John Smith, John Senhouse,
b Lawrence Standish, John Smith, Lawrence Sudel, Thomas Shepheard, Thomas Sowerbuts, Robert Sherburn, Robert Serjeant, Thomas Singleton, George Turner, John Tickle, John Tickle, Edward Tutlock, Hugh Tootle, John Tootle, Cuthbert Trelfall, Richard Thornton, John Talbot, Christopher Townley, Lawrence Stannanaught, John Turver, William Trelfal, Andrew Thistleton, William Thompson, Edward Tilsley, Edward Unsworth, Richard Urmston, George Wetherby, Richard Wadmough, Hugh Webster, Thomas Welsh, John Whittle, Thomas Woodcock, Robert Waring, Hugh Waterforth, John Westby, Francis Westby, Robert White, George Westby, John Wilkinson,
c Ralph Atterton, Samuel Clark,   Lloyd, Walter Astley, William Brand, Sir Francis Bodenham, George Brailsford, Charls Bagshaw, William Coney, John Far, Thomas Wells, Sir Philip Constable, Marmaduke Doleman, John Johnson, John Mounson, Thomas Naylor, John Plumpton, Samuel Fawcet, John Francis,   Forster, Joseph Jackman, Gabriel Sedgwick, Timothy Wright, Thomas Jones, John Lewis, William Morgan, Nathanael Prichard, John Morgan, William Flyer, William Jones, Anthony Morgan, John Morgan, Walter Norris, Thomas Stubs, Lord Charls Somerset, James Scudamore, Richard Anguish, Clippesby Bacon, William Mason, Thomas Pitcher, Sir
d Robert Winde, Edmund Mumford, John Parris, Thomas Holder, Marmaduke Moor, William Tirwhit, William Bawd, George Bartram, Thomas Clavering, Sir John Clavering, Francis Carnaby, John Fen- [220] wick, Thomas Ogle, Ralph Read, John Roddam, Musgrave Ridley, Thomas Winkle, Edward Carlton, Robert Dent, Robert Cramlington, Sir William Fenwick, Robert Fenwick, Thomas Fenwick, William Fenwick, Sir Charls Howard, Thomas Rotherford, William Swinborn, George Thirlwal, Sir Nicholas Thornton, George Wray, Sir Edward Widdrington, Ralph Widdrington, Thomas Waterton, Henry Widdrington, Henry Widdrington, Sir Charls Blount, Francis Mildmay, Richard Edwards, George Kinaston, Sir Walter Blount, Henry Englefield, Robert Baker, John Brag, William Chilcot, Richard

THIRD ACT, 1652.

a Chaffey, Samuel Chaffey, Edward Chaffey, James Dorchester, Lawrence Drake, Edward Davis, Robert Ford, Richard Gay, William Gowen, William Gaylerd, Richard Godwyn, John Hodges, Thomas Hopkins, John Horsey, Thomas Jervis, Nathanael Jones, Hugh Jones, James Moor, Richard Newcourt, William Noss, Henry Pike, William Pike, George Prater, John Roberts, John Walker, John Walcot, Richard Weech, John Wills, Humphrey Wear, Giles Pointz, Henry Fowel, Anthony Gosling, Doctor   Laney, James Mallet, John Pinchin, John Unwyn, William Budding, William Chamberlain, Thomas Chamberlain, Anthony Hide, James Linkhorn, Miles Philipson, Swithen

b Wells, Francis Collier, Dud Dudley, William Ellis, John Gifford, Sir Edward Littleton, Timothy Starting, Humphrey Vize, Thomas Wooldridge, Walter Gifford, John Gifford, Anthony Pomfret, Christopher Wheeler, Henry Bellingham, John Rigate, William Gage, Anthony Rigby, Thomas Allen, Anthony Mowsey, Henry Thynne, Francis Toop, Miles Philipson, Edmund Wells, Edward Barret, Edward Barret, Colonel Dud Dudley, Charls Kingston, Sir Edward Littleton, Thomas Warmstree, Thomas Acton, Walter Blount, Tho. Chauncey, Maj. Fredrick Winsor, Anthony Garnet, Christopher Gilpin, John Jackson, John Philipson, John Parker, Robert Pattison, John Richardson,

c Henry Salkeld, Thomas Waller, William Fleming, John Smith, Doctor   Ambrose, Thomas Awstwick, George Acklam, Adam Bland, Thomas Brockhouse, George Beesley, Richard Bowes, John Chapman, Sidney Constable, Doctor Richard Chambers, Stephen Carre, Major Lewis Carre, Henry Cholmley, Thomas Danby, William Doleman, Robert Ellis, William Flintoft, John Fleming, Robert Freer, Gabriel Freeman, William Frankland, Marmaduke Frank, William Goodman, Edward Hardcastle, George Hemsworth, John Howden, Richard Hunter, Thomas Hardwick, Thomas Hitchin, George Jackson, Christopher Kidds, Arthur Langfield, John Morley, Henry Marshal, Thomas

d Morley, John Marsh, Miles Newton, Charls North, George Noudike, John Parker, John Plumpton, John Pullen, Fairfax Ringrose, Sir John Redman, Thomas Stanley, John Smith, Sir William Theakston, Edmund Tatham, John Taylor, Richard Vincent, Stephen Whitwel, Anthony Wharton, William Winsor, Darcy Washington, James Washington, Christopher Anderton, Allen Ascough, Thomas Berney, John Adamson, James Ascough, Dame   Armitage, Henry Berney, Edward Barton, Thomas Bains, Mrs.   Butler, William Brigham, William Bulmer, William Barber, John Cansfield, John Clifton, William Constable, Matthew Constable, Marmaduke Cholmley, John Constable, Fairley Coulson, George Cockson, Philip Doleman, Marmaduke Doleman, Thomas Doleman, John Danby, Edmund Danby,

a Thomas Empson, William late Lord Ewre, William Green, Robert Gale, William Hogg, Philip Hamerton, John Hebden, Marmaduke Holtby, Peter Hawkins, John Knavesborough, Mrs.   Killingbeck, George Daniel, Richard Lowther, Richard Langley, John Middleton, Mrs.   Waterton, Nicholas Morley, Michael Metcalf, John Mallory, John Percy, Sir George Palms, Margaret Robinson, John Rider, James Robinson, Lawrence Sayer, Thomas Smith, James Singleton, William Stephenson, **Robert** Trapps, Stephen Tempest, Thomas Tankard, Charls Thimbleby, John Vavasour, Andrew Young, Bodenham Gunter, John Wintour, Dr. William Roberts, Edward Fox,
b Dr. William Lewis, John Morgan, Richard Dutton, Tristram Lloyd,   Smith, Herbert Price, John Vaughan, Tho. Bennet, John Tirer, Andrew Richards, Parris Smith, Thomas Earl of Berks, sir Thomas Chamberlain, Thomas Webb, sir Richard Titchburn, Knight and Baronet, sir Edward Plumpton, sir John Thimbleby, William Brand, Henry Fernes, Richard Witherow, Littleton Clent, sir William Quadring, Norris Fines, Henry Bidlake, Philip Philcot, George Bag, Peter Hatton, Francis Giles, John Arundel, John Portlock, Pierce Mannaton, sir Thomas Dacre, and Thomas Brockholos, or any of them, and all others claiming and to claim by, from or under them or any of
c them, or to the use of, or in Trust for them or any of them since the Twentieth day of May, One thousand six hundred forty two (and other then the Rights and Title of Dower of the respective Wife and Wives of them or any of them) All such Estates, Interests, Rents, Incumbrances, Charges, Rights in Law or Equity, which they or any of them had or ought to have had, in or to the said Manors, Lands, Tenements or Hereditaments or any of them, before the said twentieth day of May, One thousand six hundred forty two; As also all and every the Estates and Interests, Given, Granted, Demised, Allowed of or Confirmed by any Act, Order or Ordinance of Parliament, or lawfull
d Authority derived from them, unto any person or persons, Body Politique or Corporate, who have constantly adhered and been faithful unto this Parliament, and whose Estates have not otherwise been Revoked or Altered by this Parliament; If such person or persons, Body Politique or Corporate, their Heirs, Successors or Assigns, do before the First day of February, which shall be in the year One thousand six hundred fifty and two, deliver in Writing unto the Commissioners appointed by an Act, Entituled, *An Act for transferring* [221] *the Powers of the Committees for Obstructions*, or any four or more of them, a particular of such his or their Right, Title, Interest, Claim, Demand, Charge, Incumbrance or Estate in Law or Equity, and shall obtain an allowance thereof before the said Commissioners or any four

a or more of them, at or before the First day of April, which shall be in the year, of our Lord God, One thousand six hundred fifty and three; which said Commissioners are hereby appointed to be Commissioners for Removing Obstructions in the sale of all and every the premises hereby appointed to be sold, and shall have, use and exercise all and every the like Powers and Authorities in reference to the premises hereby appointed to be sold, as the said Commissioners may or ought to do in relation to the Sale of any other the Lands and Estates in an Act, Entituled, *An Act for Sale of several Lands and Estates forfeited to the Commonwealth for Treason*, mentioned; And *b* the Trustees, Treasurers, Register, Registers-Accomptant, Surveyor-General, and all other persons imployed in and about this Service, are required to observe such Orders and Directions as from time to time they shall receive from the said Commissioners; And the said Commissioners shall and may allow all incident Charges for the necessary carrying on of this Service.

And the said Trustees or any five or more of them respectively, shall and may, and are hereby Required and Authorized to Contract, Bargain, Sell, Alien and Convey all and every the said Manors and premises, and to execute all Powers and Authorities in the Sale thereof, *c* according to the Rates and Proportions, Rules and Directions limited and expressed in the said former Act, Entituled, *An Act for Sale of several Lands and Estates forfeited to the Commonwealth for Treason*, and in such maner as they may or might have done in the Sale of any the Manors or Lands vested and setled in them by the before mentioned Act.

Provided always, That the Trustees in this Act named, shall not Treat or Contract with any person or persons, Body Politique, or Corporate, for the Purchase of any Manor, Lands, Tenements or Hereditaments hereby exposed to Sale, until the expiration of thirty days next after the Return of the respective Survey and Surveys thereof.

d Provided also, and be it Enacted, and it is hereby Enacted and Declared, That it shall and may be lawful to and for any person or persons whose Estates are hereby exposed to Sale, and his and their Heirs and Assigns (notwithstanding any Clause, Article or thing in this present Act contained) to compound for any the Manors, Lands, Tenements or Hereditaments, of or belonging to such person or persons in such maner, and according to the rules and directions, and upon such conditions as are hereafter in and by this Act expressed; That is to say, All and every such person and persons, his or their Heirs or Assigns so desiring to compound, tendring unto the Commissioners named in an Act of this present Parliament, Entituled, *An Act Impowering several Commissioners to put in Execution all and every*

a the *Powers and Authorities heretofore given to the Commissioners for Compounding with Delinquents, and for managing of all Estates under Sequestration,* &c. or any four or more of them, under the hand of the Register in this Act mentioned, a true Copy of the Survey of any Manor, Lands, Tenements or Hereditaments, of or belonging to such person or persons respectively, they the said Commissioners for Compounding shall thereupon ascertain and set the Sum to be paid for such Composition at the Rates following, That is to say, For all and every such **Manor**, Lands, Tenements or Hereditaments wherein such person or persons now hath, or at the time of his death had an Estate
b of Inheritance, after the Rate of two Sixths, and so proportionably, for all and every other Estate, according to such Rules and Directions of Parliament given to the said Commissioners to be observed in the Compositions with Delinquents, accompting the clear yearly value of the premises so to be compounded for as the same are or shall be returned by the Surveyors in such Survey: And for all Timber growing or being upon the premises so to be compounded for, One full Third part of the value which by such Survey the same shall be valued at; And thereupon the said Commissioners shall send unto the Treasurers of the Receipt of Goldsmiths-Hall, a Certificate in
c writing under the hands of them the said Commissioners or any four of them, of the Sum and Sums of Money so by them ascertained and set to be paid for such Composition, together with the same Copy of the Survey whereupon such Composition shall be made; And in such case, such person and persons, his, or their Heirs or Assignes, who shall prosecute such Composition, shall pay in to the said Treasurers of the Receipt at Goldsmiths-Hall, one Moyety of the Moneys so certified, within threescore Days after such Survey shall be returned unto the Surveyor-General before-mentioned, and the other Moyety within six Moneths next after the return of the said Survey; And that upon the
d Payment of the said first Moyety, the said Treasurers shall send back unto the Trustees herein named, the same Copy of the Survey, to- [222] gether with a Certificate, under the hands of them the said Treasurers, of the Moneys so paid in upon such Composition, and that the same is the Moyety of the Sum so set for the Composition; and upon such Certificate, the said Trustees shall forbear to Treat or Contract with any person or persons for the sale of the premises so compounded for, or any part thereof; And upon payment in of the second Moyety within the six Moneths aforesaid, and Certificate thereof made by the said Treasurers to the said Commissioners for compounding, they the said Commissioners for compounding shall immediately discharge all and every the premises so compounded for, of and from Seques-

a tration; and all and every such person and persons, his and their Heirs or Assignes so compounding as aforesaid, shall from thenceforth have, hold and enjoy all and every the premises so by him compounded for, as against the Trustees in this Act named, the Survivors and Survivor of them, and his and their Heirs, in as full and ample maner as if the same had never been Vested in the said Trustees, and as if the same had not been forfeited by the Delinquency of such persons whose Estate is so compounded for as aforesaid.

And be it further Enacted by the Authority aforesaid, That all and every Papist Delinquent whose Estate is by this Act exposed to sale, *b* and who shall compound and pay in the whole Money for such Composition by the times before limited respectively, shall have liberty, and is hereby enabled, at any time within One year, to be computed from the time when the first Payment shall be so made, to Alien, Sell and Dispose of all and every the Manors, Lands, Tenements and Hereditaments so by him compounded for as aforesaid, in as full and ample maner as any other person compounding may do; But in case such Papist Delinquent shall not within the space of One year to be computed as aforesaid, depart out of this Commonwealth, and the Dominions and Territories thereunto belonging, or shall at any time *c* afterwards return into this Commonwealth, or any the Dominions or Territories thereunto belonging, That then and from thenceforth such Papist Delinquent, and all and every the Estate real and personal, whereof such Papist Delinquent, or any other person to his Use, shall at any time from and after the Expiration of the said Term of One year or of such his Return respectively be seized or possessed, shall be lyable unto the Laws touching Popish Recusants:

Provided always, That in case any person or persons aforenamed, whose Estates are hereby appointed to be sold, his or their Heirs or Assigns so compounding for any part of the premises, shall make default of Payment of the second Moyety of the Moneys so to be paid *d* upon such Composition (whereof the said Treasurers at Goldsmiths-Hall are hereby Authorized and Required to certifie the Trustees in this Act named, immediately upon such default of Payment) That then and from thenceforth the said Trustees are Authorized and Required to Treat and Contract with any other person or persons, Body Politique or Corporate for the Sale of the said premises, as if no such Composition had ever been made, nor any Money paid thereupon: And that all and every Bargains of Sale, Conveyances and Assurances to be made of any Estate or Estates in Fee-simple, or for Term of Life or Lives of any the premises, according to such Contracts as shall be agreed upon between the Purchaser or Purchasers, and the *a* said Trustees or any five or more of them respectively, shall be good and effectual in Law to all intents and purposes;

And all and every Purchaser and Purchasers of the premises or any part thereof, his and their Heirs, Successors and Assigns respectively, shall have, hold and enjoy the premises that shall be by him or them so purchased, discharged of all Trusts and Accompts whereunto the said Trustees, or any or either of them, are or may be lyable by vertue of this Act; And of all Suits and Questions that may arise or be moved upon pretence of Sale at under-values, and of all Claims and Demands whatsoever, and of all Incumbrances made by the said
b Trustees or any claiming under them or any of them; And that the same shall not be lyable unto, but freed and discharged of and from all and all maner of Statutes, Judgements, Recognizances, Dowers, Joyntures, and other Acts and Incumbrances whatsoever had, made, done or suffered, or to be had, made, done or suffered, by, from or under the said Trustees or any of them respectively, other then such Conveyances and Assurances as shall be had, made, done or suffered in performance and pursuance of the Sales and Contracts respectively made, according to the meaning of this present Act: And if any action shall be brought against the said Trustees, Treasurers or other
c Officers or Officer, or any of them, for any thing done by them or any of them in Execution of this Act, or any former Act, Ordinance, Orders or Instructions whereunto it relates, That then he or they are hereby enabled to plead the General Issue, and to give this Act in evidence; And if Judgement shall be had for the Defendant or Defendants in such action, he and they shall recover double Costs.

And whereas the Parliament do finde it necessary to raise a con- [223] siderable Sum of Money for the necessary carrying on the Services of this Commonwealth, Be it therefore Enacted and Ordained, and it is Enacted and Ordained, That the sum of Six hundred thousand Pounds
d shall be borrowed upon the security of the Lands of the said Traytors, whose Estates are by this Act appointed to be sold, by way of doubling the like Sum as is or shall be due unto any person or persons, Bodies Politique or Corporate, upon the Publique Faith, or which might have been doubled by vertue of any Act, Order or Ordinance of this present Parliament, and hath not formerly been doubled upon the Credit of Bishops and Deans and Chapters Lands, or upon the Lands of the late King, Queen and Prince, or of the Fee-farm Rents: And that all and every person and persons, Bodies Politique or Corporate, for every sum or sums of Money he or they shall further lend, may and shall be secured the Moneys formerly owing as aforesaid; And such other Moneys as he or they shall Advance for the raising of Six hundred

a thousand Pounds, upon the Lands of the said Traytors in this Act named; in such sort as by the before mentioned Act, Entituled, *An Act for the Sale of several Lands and Estates forfeited to the Commonwealth for Treason*, is Enacted or Provided; And the said Trustees are hereby Impowered and Authorized to pursue the Rules and Instructions for Doubling of Money, as is appointed and declared in the several Acts of this present Parliament for the Sale of Deans and Chapters Lands.

And be it further Enacted, That Sir John Wollaston Knight, and Alderman of the City of London, Thomas Andrews, John Dethick and *b* Francis Allein, Aldermen of the said City, shall be Treasurers for the said Service; And that they or any two of them are hereby Impowered and Authorized to receive the said Six hundred thousand pounds, and all other such sum and sums of Money as from time to time ought to be paid in to the Treasury by vertue of this Act; which shall be issued out and paid according to such Orders, Warrants, Directions, and Instructions, as they shall from time to time receive from the Parliament.

And be it further Enacted by the Authority aforesaid, That the Register in the former Act (Entituled, *An Act for the Sale of several* *c* *Lands and Estates forfeited to the Commonwealth for Treason*) and his Deputy, are hereby authorized and required upon a Warrant or Warrants from the said Trustees, to make out, rate and sign one or more Particulars of all and every the premises hereby appointed to be sold; And that the respective Trustees do upon such Particular proceed to contract with any Purchaser or Purchasers for the same, and to make sale thereof accordingly.

And be it further Enacted and Ordained, That the respective Trustees, Treasurers, Register and Surveyor-General in the said former Act for Sale of several Lands and Estates forfeited to the Common-
d wealth for Treason, shall do, execute, observe and keep all and every the like Powers, Authorities, Orders, Directions and Instructions, in relation to the premises hereby appointed to be sold, or any of them, as they and every of them ought to do or to have done in reference to other the Manors, Lands, Tenements and Hereditaments of the said Traytors and persons in the said former Act mentioned, and shall have and receive such and the like Salaries and Fees for them and their Clerks respectively, and in such sort and maner as they and every of them respectively are and ought to have and receive for their respective Services and Imployments, touching other the Manors, Lands, Tenements and Hereditaments by the said former mentioned Act appointed to be sold.

a And be it further Enacted by this present Parliament, and by Authority thereof, That all Reversions and Remainders expectant upon any Estate Tail upon any conveyance made by the said Traytor or Traytors, or any other person or persons by or under whom they or any of them claim of any the Manors, Lands, Tenements or Hereditaments of any the Traytor or Traytors in this Act, or in the aforesaid *Act for sale of several Lands and Estates forfeited to the Commonwealth for Treason* named, not actually vested in the possession of such Tenant in Tail by the death of such Traytor or Traytors before the Five and twentieth day of March, One thousand six hundred fifty *b* two, which by Fine and Recovery might be docqued by any of the said Traytor or Traytors, are and shall be to all intents and purposes forfeited for their said Treasons; And as well the said Traytors and their Heirs and Assigns, and all other persons and their Heirs in Reversion or Remainder upon any such Estate, shall be for ever barred, as if such Traytor or Traytors had actually levied a Fine, and suffered a Recovery for doing thereof, Any Allowance, Law, Statute or Usage to the contrary in any wise notwithstanding.

Provided also, That if any person or persons shall double any sum of Money upon forged Debentures, or other false Certificates, or any [224] *c* other fraudulent way or means, and thereof shall be convicted by Oath before the Commissioners for Obstructions within one year after such Doubling, every such person so offending shall forfeit treble the said sum, the one moyety thereof to the use of the Commonwealth, and the other moyety to such person or persons as shall discover the same before the said Commissioners for Obstructions in this Act named, and shall be committed to prison, and his Estate sequestred by the said Commissioners for Obstructions until payment thereof.

Provided always, and be it further Enacted, That all and every person or persons having any Estate, Right, Title or Interest of, in *d* or unto any the Lands, Tenements or Hereditaments by this Act intended or mentioned to be put to sale, or that hath any Statute, Judgement, Recognizance or Rent, which were without fraud, and for good and valuable Consideration had, made and acknowledged before any Treason respectively committed by any of the persons in this Act named, whose Estates are appointed to be sold; and shall obtain an allowance thereof by the said Commissioners for removing of Obstructions before the First day of January, One thousand six hundred fifty two, That then the same shall be good and effectual to such person or persons, their Executors, Administrators and Assigns respectively, to all intents and purposes, according to the tenor thereof, Any thing in this Act to the contrary in any wise notwithstanding.

a Provided nevertheless, and it is further Enacted, That in recompence and satisfaction of such Judgements, Statutes, Recognizances, Mortgages, and other Incumbrances, as by the true intent and provision of this Act are to be satisfyed, the said Trustees or any five or more of them upon the return of the respective Surveys, are hereby impowered and authorized to set out such proportion of Lands so surveyed, as will be sufficient to satisfy such Incumbrance and Incumbrances; And after such Incumbrances proved, and the Debts allowed of by the Commissioners for removing of Obstructions, to sell and convey such proportionable part of the said
b Lands so surveyed, to such Creditor or Creditors or their Assigns, in recompence and satisfaction of such Incumbrance and Incumbrances, either for Life, Lives, Years or in Fee, the said Trustees taking care in satisfying such Incumbrances to satisfie the same in such priority and course as the same ought to be satisfied by the Laws of this Land; And upon such Conveyance and Conveyances made, the said Creditor and Creditors, their Heirs, Executors, Administrators or Assigns shall acknowledge satisfaction upon Record, or otherwise release and discharge such Judgements, Statutes, Recognizances, Mortgages and other Incumbrances respectively, as the Council of the
c said Trustees, and for the Commonwealth shall direct and advise; And such Acknowledgement, Release and Discharge shall be good and effectual in Law to discharge the said Debts and Incumbrances, as against the residue of the said Lands intended to be sold by this Act, Any Law, Statute or Usage to the contrary in any wise notwithstanding.

Provided always, and be it Enacted by the Authority aforesaid, That the aforesaid Trustees and their Heirs, and the Heirs of the Survivors and Survivor of them, shall and do stand seized of so much of the Manors, Lands, Tenements and Hereditaments of the Traytors
d aforesaid in this Act named, as shall and doth amount to the full and clear yearly value of Ten thousand Pounds by the year, to the Trusts and Uses limited and appointed in and by the aforesaid Act, Entituled, *An Act for the Sale of several Lands and Estates forfeited to the Commonwealth for Treason*, to make up and supply what their former Security in and by the said Act is or shall be weakned, by the taking away out of the said Lands by the Act exposed to sale, any Lands by Acts of Parliament setled on any person or persons whatsoever.

Provided always, and be it Enacted, That such of the Traytors in this Act named as shall be certified by the Commissioners for compounding to the Trustees aforesaid, to have committed any Act of *a* Treason or Rebellion since the Thirtieth of January, One thousand six hundred forty eight, such Traytor or Traytors shall in no wise have or enjoy any benefit or advantage of any Clause for Compounding, but his or their Estates shall be sold as confiscate to the use of the Commonwealth, Any thing in this Act to the contrary in any wise notwithstanding.

Provided alwaies, and be it Enacted, That if it shall appear to the Commissioners for compounding before the First day of February, One thousand six hundred fifty two, that any of the persons whose names are inserted, and Estates exposed to sale by this Act, were not *b* by Authority of Parliament upon the First day of December, One thousand six hundred fifty one, under Actual sequestration for bearing of arms against the Parliament, or for assisting or adhering to the Enemies thereof in the late Wars, or who having been sequestred [225] have compounded for their Delinquency, and received a Discharge for the same by any authorized by Parliament thereunto, shall be and is hereby declared to be exempted out of this Act, to all intents and purposes, as if such persons name had not been inserted in this Act, Any thing to the contrary in any wise notwithstanding: And upon a Certificate thereof from the said Commissioners to the Trustees and *c* Contractors in this Act named, the said Trustees and Contractors are hereby required to forbear all Proceedings therein against any such persons by themselves or any other Officers under them.

And be it further Enacted by the Authority aforesaid, That Philip Tandy, William Benson and Edward Green, be and are hereby constituted and appointed Register-Accomptant, and shall have and execute the Office of Register-Accomptant in the sale of the Lands of the late Archbishops, Bishops, Deans and Chapters, Gleab-Lands, Fee-farm Rents, and of several Lands and Estates forfeited to the Commonwealth for Treason, by this present Act or by former Acts *d* exposed to sale; as also of Register-Accomptant for the sum of Two hundred and two and forty thousand pounds doubled at Weavers-Hall; and shall do, execute, observe and keep all and every the like Powers, Authorities, Orders, Directions and Instructions, in relation to all and every the premises, or any of them, as the Register-Accomptant named in any Act or Ordinance of Parliament concerning any of the premises ought to do, or to have done in reference to the premises or any of them respectively; and also that they or any two of them, whereof the said Philip Tandy to be one, shall examine and approve of all Debentures, before the same be allowed by the respective Trustees for sale of the premises or any of them, and shall observe such Orders and Directions as they shall from time to time *a* receive from the Commissioners for removing Obstructions in this Act before mentioned.

And be it further Enacted by the Authority aforesaid, That a Certificate under the hands of the said Philip Tandy, William Benson and Edward Green, or any two of them, whereof the said Philip Tandy to be one, shall be a sufficient Voucher unto the Treasurers of the respective Offices, to proceed thereupon to the receiving of the Money or Bills doubled upon any of the Securities, according to the former Acts and Ordinances of Parliament in that behalf; And that the said Philip Tandy, William Benson and Edward Green, for their said
b Service in all and every the premises, shall have, and be allowed the yearly Salary of Six hundred pounds, to be equally divided between them, for themselves and their Clerks, payable quarterly by the Treasurers for Sale of the several Lands and Estates forfeited to the Commonwealth for Treason.

Provided always, That in case the persons whose names are inserted in this Act, who have paid the first Moyety of their Fines for their Compositions for Delinquency, shall at or before the First day of February, One thousand six hundred fifty two, pay unto the Treasurers at Goldsmiths-Hall, the latter Moyety of their Fines, with Damages
c for the Forbearance thereof from the time the same should have been paid, at the rate of Eight pounds in the Hundred before the Statute, and six pounds since, the same shall be accepted, and that upon Certificate of the said Treasurers to the Commissioners for Compounding, of such Payment made by the time aforesaid, the said Commissioners for Compounding are hereby authorized and required to discharge the Sequestration of such person so making payment as aforesaid; And that all and every such person and persons be, and are hereby Declared to be Freed and Discharged from thenceforth of his and their Delinquency: And that all and every such person and
d persons, his and their Heirs and Assigns shall from thenceforth have, hold and enjoy all his and their Estates as fully and amply, as if his and their Names had never been inserted into this Act, Any thing in this present Act to the contrary in any wise notwithstanding.

And be it Enacted by the Authority aforesaid, That Randal Manwaring Gentleman, be and is hereby constituted and appointed Comptroller of all Entries, Receipts and Payments which shall be made to or by the Treasurers aforesaid, and shall have Power and Authority, by himself or his sufficient Deputies, to keep Accompt of all Entries, Receipts, Payments and Discompts whatsoever, which shall be made unto or by the Treasurers; and that the Comptroller or his Deputies shall execute the said place of Comptroller in relation to the premises, *a* as also in relation to the sale of all and every the Lands and Estates exposed to sale by a former Act of this present Parliament, Entituled, *An Act for Sale of several Lands and Estates forfeited to the Commonwealth for Treason;* As also by another Act of this present Parliament, Entituled, *An Act for several Lands and Estates forfeited to the Commonwealth for Treason, appointed to be sold for the use of the Navy;* according to such Instructions and Directions as the Comptroller in the said former Acts or either of them ought to do or to have done; [226] and shall receive the Fee and yearly Salary of Two hundred Pounds by like quarterly Payments as is appointed by the said former Act, in *b* full satisfaction of him and his Clerks, for his and their service in the place of Comptroller, both in **this** and **the** two former Acts.

Passed 18 *November.*

INDEX.

Abbots-An, Hampshire (Fowel) 47*b*
Abergavenny, Monmouthshire (Prichard) . . 45*c*
Abraham, Lancashire (Leyland) 41*b*
ACKLAM, George, of Bewholm, Yorkshire . . 48*b*
ACTON, Thomas, of Bourton (or Burton), Worcestershire 40*d*; 48*a*
Acton, Staffordshire (Wooldridge) . . . 47*c*
ADAMSON, John, of Thornton, Yorkshire . . . 49*c*
Adlington, Cheshire (Leighe) 38*c*
Adlington, Lancashire (Norris) 43*c*
Akeham-Grange, Yorkshire (Gale) . . . 50*a*
Alcliff, Lancashire (Serjeant) 44*b*
Alker, Lancashire (Gore) 42*c*
———————— (Lovelady) 43*a*
———————— (Tickle) 44*c*
ALLANSON, Sir William, Knight . . . 5*d*
Allein, Francis, Alderman of London . 5*c*; 14*d*; 34*b*; 65*b*
ALLEN, Thomas, of Laystuff, co. Suffolk, Mariner . . 47*d*
ALLENSON, William, of Woolton-magna, co. Lancaster . 41*a*
Allerton, Lancashire (Lathom) 43*a*
Altham, Lancashire (Par) 43*d*
Althorn, Essex (Anderton) 40*b*
Alvington, Gloucestershire 27*b*
AMBROSE, Doctor ——, of Sheepley, Yorkshire . . 48*b*
Ammersden, Oxfordshire (Mildmay) . . . 46*c*
Amotherby, Yorkshire (Ringrose) . . . 49*a*
ANDERTON, ——, of Althorn, Essex . . . 40*b*
ANDERTON, Christopher, of Anderton, Essex . . 49*b*
ANDERTON, Hugh, of Euxton, co. Lancaster . . 41*d*
ANDERTON, James, of Birchley in Billing, co. Lancaster . 41*d*
ANDERTON, James, of Clayton, co. Lancaster . . 41*d*
ANDERTON, William, of Anderton, co. Lancaster . . 41*d*

Anderton, co. Lancaster (Anderton) . . . 41*d*
Anderton, Yorkshire (Anderton) . . . 49*b*
ANDREWS, Thomas . . . 14*d*; 34*b*; 65*a*
ANGUISH, Richard, of Scarming, co. Norfolk . . 45*d*
ANNE, Philip, of Burwallis . . . 30*b*
Armingland, Manor of, Norfolk (Fleetwood) . . 21*a*
ARMITAGE, Dame ——, of Herthead, co. York . . 49*c*
ARNOLD, William, of Crosby, co. Lancaster . . 41*a*
ARUNDEL, Henry, Lord, Baron of Warder . . 40*a*
ARUNDEL, John, of Sithney, co. Cornwall . . 51*b*
ARUNDEL, Richard, of Walkampton, co. Devon . . 39*b*
ASCOUGH, Allen, of Skewsby, co. York . . 49*b*
ASCOUGH, James, of Dinsdale, co. York . . 49*c*
ASCOUGH, James, of Middleton on Rowe, co. Durham . 39*d*
ASH, Edward, ... 5*c*
Ash, Kent (Nethersole) 41*a*
Ashley, Lancashire (Tilsley) . . . 44*d*
ASHTON, Henry, of Blackrod, co. Lancaster . . 42*a*
Ashton, Lancashire (Gerrard) . . . 42*d*
ASTLEY, Walter, of Pascal, co. Stafford . . 45*a*
ASTON, Sir Arthur, of Oxford (Knight) . . . 2*d*
ASTON, Sir Thomas, of Aston (Baronet), co. Chester . 38*a*
Aston, co. Chester (Aston) 38*a*
ATTERTON, Ralph, of Newbold, co. Leicester . . 45*a*
Awdfield, Yorkshire (Smith) 49*b*
AWSTWICK, Thomas, of Pomfret, co. York . . 48*b*
Awton, Lancashire (Welsh) . . . 44*d*
AYRE, Rowland, of Hassop, co. Derby . . . 2*d*

BACON, Clippesby, of Corpusty, co. Norfolk . . 45*d*
Badsworth, Yorkshire (Dolman) . . . 30*b*
BAG, George, of ——, co. Devon . . . 51*a*
BAGSHAW, Charles, of Bourn, co. Lincoln . . 45*a*
Bail, The, Lincolnshire (Nayler) . . . 45*b*
BAINS, Thomas, of Sellet, co. Lancaster . . 42*b*
BAINS, Thomas, of Twisleton, co. York . . 49*c*
BAKER, John 16*a*
BAKER, Robert, of Minehead, co. Somerset . . 46*c*
BAMBER, John, of Layton, co. Lancaster . . 42*a*
Bankhouse, Yorkshire (Cockson) . . . 49*d*
BARBER, William, of Clint, Yorkshire . . . 49*c*
BARKER, Alexander, of Dalton, Lancashire . . 42*a*

BARKER, John, of Weetley, Lancashire	41*a*
Barking, Essex (Fanshaw)	40*c*
BARNET, John, of Sound, in the Parish of Wrenbury, Cheshire	38*b*
Barnets-wood	27*c*
BARNS, Thomas, of Goose-nargh cum Whittingham, Lancashire	41*a*
BARRET, Sir Edward, of Droitwich, Worcestershire.	47*d*
BARRET, Edward, of Droitwich, Worcestershire	47*d*
BARRET, Edward, junior, of Droitwich, Worcestershire	47*d*
Barrow, Somerset (Doddington)	1*a*
BARTON, Edward, of Towthorp, Yorkshire	49*c*
Barton, Manor of, *alias* Pentherry, Monmouthshire.	27*b*
BARTRAM, George, of Elswick, co. Northumberland	45*d*
BAWD, William, of Walgrave, co. Nottingham	45*d*
Beamish, Durham (Wray)	40*a*
BEAMONT, Rice, of Egermon, co. Cumberland	38*c*
BEAR, Nicholas, of Silferton, co. Devon	39*b*
BECKWITH, Thomas, of Beverley, Yorkshire	2*d*
Bedd' (Shuttleworth)	44*a*
BEDDINFIELD, Sir Henry, of co. of Norfolk (Knight)	2*d*
BEESLEY, George, of Twisleton, Yorkshire	48*c*
BEESLY, Thomas, of Layton and Boughton, Lancashire	41*a*
Beeston, Cheshire (Parsons)	38*c*
Befront, Northumberland (Errington)	30*b*
BELLINGHAM, Henry, of Newtimber, co. Sussex	47*d*
BENION, (Sir) George, of Mussel Hill, co. Middlesex	2*b*
BENNET, Thomas, Cheshire	50*d*
Benningholm-Grange, Yorkshire (Constable)	49*d*
Bennyfield-Lawn, Northamptonshire (Hatton)	2*c*
BENSON, William	68*c*
Bentley, Sussex (Gage)	47*d*
BERKS, Thomas, Earl of	50*d*
BERNEY, Henry, of Haddockstone, Yorkshire	49*c*
BERNEY, Thomas, of Dolebank, Yorkshire	49*c*
BERRY, John, of Haughton, Lancashire	42*a*
Berwick upon Tweed	6*d*
Bettus and Perlloyd, Lands and Tenements called, Monmouthshire	26*a*
Beverley, Yorkshire (Beckwith)	2*d*
Bewholm, Yorkshire (Acklam)	48*b*
Bickerstaff, Lancashire (Mossock)	43*c*
——————— (Stanley)	44*b*
Biddeston, Wilts (Thynne)	47*d*
BIDDULPH, Francis, of Biddulph (Staffordshire)	30*b*

BIDDULPH, John, of Biddulph, Staffordshire . . 38c
Biddulph, Staffordshire (Francis Biddulph) . . 30b
———————— (John Biddulph) . . 38c
BIDLAKE, Henry, of Bridstow or Briddestow, Devonshire 39b; 51a
Biggin, Yorkshire (Hardcastle) . . . 48d
Biker, Northumberland (Dent) . . . 46a
Billington, Lancashire (Craven) . . . 41a
———————— (Fowl) 42c
Birchley in Billing, Lancashire (Anderton) . . 41d
BIRTWISLE, Thomas, of Huncoat, Lancashire . . 42a
Bisciter, Oxfordshire (Blount) . . . 46c
Bishop-Mouncton, Yorkshire (Pullen) . . . 49a
Bishops Candle, Dorset 22c
Bishops-frome, Herefordshire (Slaughter) . . 40d
Bishopton, Yorkshire (Stanley) . . . 49b
Blackrod, Lancashire (Martingdal) . . . 41c
———————— (Ashton) . . . 42a
———————— (Janyon) . . . 43a
———————— (Norris) 43c
Blagden, Northumberland (Fenwick) . . . 46b
BLAGRAVE, Daniel 5c
BLAND, Adam, Yorkshire 48b
BLAND, Sir Thomas, of Skippar, Yorkshire . . 48b
Blendworth, Manor of, Southampton, co. Southampton . 26d
Blisland, Cornwall (Spry) 38a
BLOUNT, Sir Charles, of Bisciter, Oxfordshire . . 46c
BLOUNT, Sir Walter, of Mawley, Salop . . . 46c
BLOUNT, Walter, of Soddington, Worcestershire . . 48a
BLUNDEL, Robert, of Ince Blundel, Lancashire . . 30a
BLUNDEL, William, of Crosby-Parva, Lancashire . . 42a
BODENHAM, Sir Francis, of Roel, Rutlandshire . . 45a
BODENHAM, Roger, of Rotheras, Herefordshire . . 2d
BODVILE, John 2a
Bold, Lancashire (Jackson) 43a
BOND, Denis 5c
BOND, John, of Inkling-Green, Lancashire . . 41a
Bootland, Northumberland (Widdrington) . . 46c
BOOTLE, Robert, of Thornton, Lancashire . . 42a
BOSTOCK, Edward, of Harup (Yeoman), Cheshire . 38b
Botsford, Lincolnshire (Doleman) . . . 45b
Boughton, (Beesly) Lancashire . . . 41a
BOURCHIER, Sir John (Knight) . . . 5c

Bourn, Lincolnshire (Bagshaw)	45*a*
Bourton, Worcestershire (Acton)	48*a*
Bowerhouse, Lancashire (Green)	42*d*
Bowes, Richard, of York	48*c*
Bowyet, Hampshire (Linkhorn)	47*c*
Boynton, Sir Matthew, of Scarborough, Yorkshire.	1*b*
Bradkirk, Lancashire (Parker).	43*d*
Bradley, James, of Bryning, Lancashire.	41*a*
Bradley, Lancashire (Eyves)	42*c*
Bradshaw, John, of Scale, Lancashire	42*b*
Bradway, Dorsetshire (Samwaies)	40*b*
Braithwait, Thomas, of Neesam Abby, Yorkshire.	39*d*
Brag, John, of Crewkhern, Somersetshire	46*c*
Brailsford, George, of Harlaxden, Lincolnshire	45*a*
Brambleshom, Lancashire (Greehalgh)	41*b*
Bramham, Yorkshire (Goodman)	48*d*
Bramwich, Yorkshire (Goodman)	48*d*
Brand, William, Lincolnshire.	51*a*
Brand, William, of Horncastle, Lincolnshire	45*a*
Bransby, Yorkshire (Cholmley)	49*d*
Brentford, Middlesex (Forster)	45*b*
Brereton, Sir William	5*c*
Brereton, Cheshire (Robinson)	38*c*
Bressencoat, Derbyshire (Merry)	39*b*
Brestwick, Northumberland (Fenwick)	46*b*
Bretherton, Lancashire (Robinson) (Snart)	41*c*; 41*d*
Bretland, John, of Thorncliff (Cheshire)	38*b*
Briddestow, Devonshire (Bidlake)	51*a*
Bridge-water, Somersetshire (Jones)	47*a*
Bridstow, Devonshire (Bidlake)	39*b*
Brigham, William, of Wilton, Yorkshire.	49*c*
Brindle, Lancashire (Woodcock)	44*d*
Brinscals, Lancashire (Haughton)	41*b*
Brinton, Huntingdonshire (Knights)	38*a*
Bristol, John, Earl of	1*a*; 22*d*; 25*c*
Broad Street, in the City of London (Fawcet)	45*b*
Brockholes, Thomas, of Cheyley, Lancashire	42*a*
Brockholes, Thomas, of Hayton, Lancashire	42*a*
Brockholes, Thomas, of Heaton, Lancashire	51*b*
Brockhouse, Thomas, of Grimlington, co. Westmerland	48*b*
Bromham, Bedford (Dives)	1*b*
Brook, Thomas, of Madely, Shropshire	30*b*

Brown, John	5c
Brown, John, of Standish, Lancashire	42a
Broxton, Cheshire (Dod)	38b
Bruton, Somersetshire (Jervis)	46d
Bryning, Lancashire (Bradley)	41a
Buckingham, George, Duke of	1a; 21d; 25b
Budding, William, of Clinton, co. Southampton (Husbandman)	47b
Budworth, Little, Cheshire (Walker)	38c
Bulmer, Anthony, of Ketton, co. Durham	39d
Bulmer, William, of Marrick, Yorkshire	49c
Bunch, James (late Alderman), of London	2a
Burlase, Nicholas, of Treludda, co. Cornwall	38a
Burleton, Richard, of Stalbridge, co. Dorset	40a
Burrowby, Yorkshire (Danby)	49d
Burscoe, Lancashire (Fletcher)	42c
Burton, Worcestershire (Acton)	40d
Burton, Yorkshire (Morley)	49a
Burwallis, Yorkshire (Anne)	30b
Burwardsley, Cheshire (Hodgkey)	38c
Butler, Mrs. ——, of Grisby, Yorkshire	49c
Butler, Edward, of Outrawcliff, Lancashire	42a
Butler, Henry, of Goosenargh cum Whittingham, Lancashire	42a
Butler, William, of Mierscough, Lancashire	42b
Buttersett, Yorkshire (Tankard)	50c
Byron, Sir John, of Newsted-Abby, Nottinghamshire, Knight	1a
Cadwel, Cumberland (Musgrave)	1a
Calcley, Northumberland (Clavering)	45d
Calvert, John, of Cockerum (Lancashire)	42b
Cambridge, Earl of, (commonly called Duke Hamilton)	2d
Candle-wake, Dorset (or Bishop's Candle)	22c
Cansfield, Sir John, of ——, Yorkshire	49c
Cansfield, John, of, ——, Yorkshire	49c
Carew, John	5b
Carlisle (Lodowick West, Prebend)	39a
Carlton, Edward, of Hesleside, co. Northumberland	46a
Carlton, Yorkshire (Thimbleby)	50c
Carnaby, Francis, of Cogston, co. Northumberland	46a
Carperby, Yorkshire (Hawkins)	50a
Carraw, Northumberland (Waterton)	46b
Carre, Lewis, Major, of Lowkellerbey, Yorkshire	48c
Carre, Stephen, of Sandisk, Yorkshire (Yeoman)	48c

INDEX. 77

Carre, Yorkshire (Danby)	48c
CARTER, Joseph, of Furnes, Lancashire	41a
CARTER, Richard, of Widnes, Lancashire.	42b
CARTERET, Sir Philip, Knight	2a
CARTERET, Philip	2a
Cartington, Northumberland (Widdrington)	46b
Casebuchan, Monmouthshire (Morgan)	45c
CASTLEHAVEN, James, Earl of	2a
Catherinton, Manor of, co. Southampton	26d
Cuttam, Suffolk (Mowsey)	47d
Catteral, Lancashire (Clark)	42b
Causeway in Roddipol, Dorsetshire (Pain)	40b
Cavan, Cornwall (Langdon)	38a
CHAFFEY, Edward, of Stoak under Hambden, Somersetshire	46d
CHAFFEY, Richard, of Stoak under Hambden, Somersetshire	46c
CHAFFEY, Samuel, of Mountague, Somersetshire (Free-mason).	46d
CHALLONER, James	5d
CHALLONER, Thomas	5b
Chalton, Manor of, co. Southampton (*alias* Chanton)	26d
CHAMBERLAIN, Sir Thomas, of Oxon (Baronet)	50d
CHAMBERLAIN, Thomas, of Lindhurst, co. Southampton	47b
CHAMBERLAIN, William, of Nash, co. Southampton	47b
CHAMBERS, Doctor Richard, Yorkshire	48c
CHANING, John, Lieut., late of Froom, Vawchurch, co. Dorset.	25b
Chanton, Manor of, co. Southampton (*alias* Chalton)	26d
CHANTREL, Robert, of Knoetorum cum Woodchurch, Cheshire.	38c
CHAPMAN, John, of Hurwoodale, Yorkshire	48c
CHARNOCK, Thomas, of Lidney, Gloucestershire	40c
CHAUNCEY, Thomas, of Kittermister, Worcestershire	48a
Chepstow, Monmouthshire	27b; 27c
Chepstow Grange, Monmouthshire	27c
Chepstow, Manor of, Monmouthshire	27b
Cherryorton, Huntingdonshire (Prat)	40d
Chester (Gamul)	38b
CHESTERFIELD, Philip, Earl of	2c
Cheyley, Lancashire (Brockholes)	42a
CHILCOT, William, of Milverton, Somersetshire	46c
Chillingham, Northumberland (Grey)	2c
Chillington, Staffordshire (Gifford)	30b
Chipping, Lancashire (Perkinson)	41c
——————————— (Harris).	42d
Chirton, Northumberland (Read)	46a

Chisleborough, Somersetshire (Wills)	47*a*
Cholmley, Henry, of Tunstal, Yorkshire.	48*c*
Cholmley, Marmaduke, of Bransby, Yorkshire	49*d*
Chorley, Richard, of Chorley, Lancashire	**42*b***
Chorley, Robert, of Yealand, Lancashire	**42*b***
Chorley, Lancashire (Melling).	41*c*
———————— (Chorley).	42*b*
———————— (Gellibrand)	42*d*
———————— (Tootle) .	44*c*
———————— (Waring)	44*d*
Cirencester, Gloucestershire (Portlock) . . . 40*c*;	51*b*
Clains, Worcestershire (Winsor)	48*a*
Clanfield, Manor of, co. Southampton	26*d*
Clark, Ralph, of Frognal, co. Kent	41*a*
Clark, Samuel, of Kingsthorp, co. Northampton	45*a*
Clark, Thomas, of Catteral, Lancashire .	42*b*
Clavering, Sir John, of Caleley, co. Northumberland (Knight).	45*d*
Clavering, Thomas, of Learchild, co. Northumberland	45*d*
Clawton, Lancashire (Parkinson)	**43*d***
Clayton, Lancashire (Anderton)	41*d*
———————— (Grimshaw)	42*d*
Clement, Gregory .	5*c*
Clent, Littleton, of Knightwick, Worcestershire	51*a*
Clerk, James, of Ilford, co. Essex	40*c*
Cleveland, Thomas, Earl of .	2*a*
Cliff, John, of Eccleston, Lancashire .	42*b*
Cliff Park, Northampton (Shepheard)	40*d*
Clifton, Jervase, of Salming Grange, Lancashire	42*b*
Clifton, John, of Worsal, Yorkshire (Yeoman)	49*d*
Clifton, Thomas, of Litham, Lancashire .	30*a*
Clint, Yorkshire (Barber)	49*c*
———————— (Hebden)	50*a*
Clinton, Hampshire (Budding)	47*b*
Clowerwal, Gloucestershire (Throgmorton)	40*c*
Coaton, Staffordshire (Ellis) .	47*c*
Coatsworth, Ralph, of Great Stainton, co. Durham	39*d*
Cockerum, Lancashire (Calvert)	42*b*
Cockson, George, of Bankhouse, Yorkshire	49*d*
Coggan, Andrew, of Greenwich, co. Kent (Merchant)	2*b*
Cogston, Northumberland (Carnaby)	46*a*
Colchester, Essex (Norton)	40*c*
Collier, Francis, of Stone, Staffordshire.	47*c*

COLLINGWOOD, Cuthbert, of Dawden, co. Durham	39*d*
COLLINS, George, of Helston, co. Cornwall	38*a*
Colton, Yorkshire (Ratcliff)	1*b*
Colwel, Northumberland (Widdrington)	46*b*
Combe-Pine, Devonshire (Cox)	39*b*
Compton-Dundon, Somersetshire (Horsey)	46*d*
CONEY, William, of Stoak, Lincolnshire	45*a*
Congleton, Cheshire (Green)	38*b*
CONINGSBY, Thomas, of North-mims (Hertfordshire)	40*d*
Conow, Lancashire (Smith)	44*b*
CONSTABLE, John, of Kirby-Knowl, Yorkshire	49*d*
CONSTABLE, Matthew, of Benningholm-grange, Yorkshire	49*d*
CONSTABLE, Sir Philip, of Middle-Rason, Lincolnshire	45*b*
CONSTABLE, Sidney, of Sherburn, Yorkshire	48*c*
CONSTABLE, Sir William, Baronet	5*c*
CONSTABLE, William, of Kathorp, Yorkshire	49*d*
CONWEL, George, of Watton, Lancashire	42*b*
CONYERS, Katherine, of ——, co. Durham	39*c*
COOK, Thomas, of Gray's Inn, co. Middlesex	30*a*
COPLESTONE, John, of Nash, co. Dorsetshire	40*a*
Coppul, Lancashire (Pilkington)	41*c*
Corpusty, Norfolk (Bacon)	45*d*
CORBET, John	5*b*
COTTAM, Richard, of Dilworth, Lancashire	42*b*
COTTINGTON, Francis, Lord	.1*b*; 45*b*
COULSON, Fairley, of Libberston, Yorkshire, Yeoman	49*d*
Covent-garden, Middlesex (Jackman)	45*b*
Cowbridge, Glamorganshire (Jenkin)	2*c*
Cox, John, of Combe-Pine, Yeoman, Devonshire	39*b*
CRAMLINGTON, Robert, of Newsham, co. Northumberland	46*a*
CRAVEN, William, Lord	30*a*
CRAVEN, Robert, of Billington, Lancashire	41*a*
Crewkhern, Somersetshire (Brag)	46*c*
———————— (Ford)	46*d*
Croglin, Cumberland (Howard)	39*a*
CROMWELL, Oliver	26*b*; 28*a*
Crookden, Northumberland (Fenwick)	46*a*
Crookham, Manor of, Berkshire	26*b*
Cropton, Yorkshire (Whitwel)	49*b*
Crosby, Lancashire (Arnold)	41*a*
Crosby-magna, Lancashire (Rice)	43*d*
Crosby-Parva, Lancashire (Blundel)	42*a*

Crosby-Parva, Lancashire (Rice)	44*a*
Crosby-Ravenwich, Westmerland (Richardson)	48*b*
CROSLAND, Jordan, of Furnes, Lancashire	42*b*
Croston, Lancashire (Wright)	41*d*
———— (Naylor)	43*c*
———— (Rutter)	44*a*
Crymlands	26*b*
Crymland, Manor of, co. Monmouth	27*b*
Cudderstone, Somerset (Stowel)	1*a*
Cuesdal, Lancashire (Park)	41*c*
Culhampton, Devonshire (Moor)	39*c*
CULPEPPER, Sir John, of Hollingborn, co. Kent (Knight)	1*a*
Curre, Lancashire (Townley)	44*c*
Curringham, Essex (Shelton, *alias* Sheldon)	40*c*
DACRE, Sir Thomas, of Levercust, co. Cumberland (Knight)	51*b*
DALTON, Thomas, of Turnham, Lancashire	42*c*
Dalton, Lancashire (Barker)	42*a*
Dalton in Furnes, Lancashire (Roscoe)	44*a*
Dalton, North, Yorkshire (Langdale)	1*a*
DANBY, Edmund, of Burrowby, Yorkshire	49*d*
DANBY, John, of Leak, Yorkshire	49*d*
DANBY, Thomas, **of Carre**, Yorkshire	48*c*
DANIEL, George, of Thorp, Brantington, Yorkshire	50*a*
DARNAL, Ralph	9*a*; 11*b*
Darrashal, Northumberland (Ogle)	46*a*
DARWEN, William, of Wavertree, Lancashire	41*b*
DAVIS, Edward, of Lamyet, Somersetshire	46*d*
Dawden, Durham (Collingwood)	39*d*
Dendron in Furnes, Lancashire (Singleton)	44*b*
DENHAM, Sir John, Knight (Baron of the Court of Exchequer)	2*c*
DENHAM, John	29*a*
DENHAM, John, of Egham, co. Surrey	2*c*
DENT, Robert, of Biker, co. Northumberland	46*a*
DENTON, Edward, of Ditton, Lancashire	42*b*
DENTON, John, of Widnes, Lancashire	41*a*
Denton, East, Northumberland (Errington)	30*a*
DERBY, James, Earl of	1*b*; 50*d*
Derby (Moor)	43*b*
———— (Serjeant)	44*a*
———— (Standish)	44*b*
———— (Tickle)	44*c*

Dethick, John (Alderman)	14d; 34b; 65a
Detton, Shropshire (Englefield)	46c
Digby, George, Lord	1a; 22d; 25c
Dilston, Northumberland (Ratcliff)	30b
Dilworth, Lancashire (Cottam)	42b
Dimples, Lancashire (Pleshington)	43d
Dingastow, Monmouthshire (Jones)	30a
Dinkley, Lancashire (Talbot)	44c
Dinsdale, Yorkshire (Ascough)	49c
Ditton, Lancashire (Denton)	42b
Dives, Sir Lewis, of Bromham, Bedfordshire (Knight)	1b
Dobson, Hugh, of Legrum, Lancashire	42c
Docker, Lancashire (North)	43c
Dod, Pierce, of Broxton (Cheshire)	38b
Doddington, Sir Francis, of Barrow, Somersetshire (Knight)	1a
Doddleston, co. Chester (Hope)	38b
Dolebank, Yorkshire (Berney)	49c
Doleman, Marmaduke, of Botsford, Lincolnshire	45b
Doleman, Marmaduke, of Middleton, Yorkshire	49d
Doleman, Philip, of ——, Yorkshire	49d
Doleman, Thomas, of Duncoats, Yorkshire	49d
Doleman, William, of Duncoats, Yorkshire	48c
Dolman, Robert, of Badsworth, Yorkshire	30b
Dorchester, James, of Puckington, Somersetshire	46d
Dormer, John	5b
Doughty, Henry, of Thornley, Lancashire	41b
Downs, John	5c
Drake, Lawrence, of Isle Abbots, Somersetshire	46d
Droitwich, Worcestershire (Barret)	47d
Dudley, Dud, Colonel, of Dudley, Worcestershire	47d
Dudley, Dud, of Greenlodge, Staffordshire	47c
Dudley, Worcestershire (Colonel Dud Dudley)	47d
Dunbar, Viscount, of Holderness, Yorkshire	30c
Duncoats, Yorkshire (William Doleman)	48c
Duncoats, Yorkshire (Thomas Doleman)	49d
Durham (Power)	40a
Dutton, Richard, of Kefennern, Flintshire	50d
Dutton, Cheshire (Harper)	38b
Eastbury, Berkshire (Gifford)	38a
Eastly, Hampshire (Wells)	47c
Eastquantonhead, Somersetshire (Hodges)	46d

82   ROYALIST CONFISCATION ACTS.

Eastwick, Shropshire (Kinaston)	46c
Eccleston, Lancashire (Cliff)	42b
——————— (Howard)	42d
——————— (Senhouse)	44b
——————— (Webster)	44d
Eccleston Magna, Lancashire (Thompson)	44d
Ednol, Cumberland (Storey)	39a
EDWARDS, Humphry.	5b
EDWARDS, Richard	5b
EDWARDS, Richard, of Pentrewarn, Shropshire	46c
Egermon, Cumberland (Beamont)	39a
EGERTON, Richard, of Ridley, Cheshire	38b
Egham, Surrey (Denham)	2c
Egton, Yorkshire (Smith)	50b
Ellel, Lancashire (Preston)	43d
ELLIS, Robert, Paulharburn, Yorkshire	39c
ELLIS, Robert, of Towthorp, Yorkshire	48c
ELLIS, William	5c
ELLIS, William, of Coaton, Staffordshire.	47c
Elton, Durham (Errington)	39d
ELTONHEAD, Richard, junior, of Eltonhead, Lancashire	42c
Eltonhead, Lancashire (Eltonhead)	42c
Elswick, Northumberland (Bartram)	45d
Elwick, Durham (Sherratton)	40a
EMERSON, Robert, of Ludwel, co. Durham	39c
EMPSON, Thomas, of Goul, Yorkshire	49d
ENGLEFIELD, Henry, of Detton, Shropshire	46c
Engleton, Yorkshire (Lowther)	50a
Ennington, Hampshire (Unwin)	47b
Eppleby, Yorkshire (Wharton)	49b
Epworth, Lincolnshire (Farr)	45a
ERRINGTON, Henry, of Befront, co. Northumberland	30b
ERRINGTON, John, of Elton, co. Durham	39d
ERRINGTON, John, of Rudby, Yorkshire	39d
ERRINGTON, Lancelot, of East Denton, co. Northumberland	30a
Errington, Nicholas, of Pont Island, co. Northumberland	30a
Eshur, Surrey (Pomfret)	47d
Euxton, Lancashire (Anderton)	41d
——————— (Smith)	44b
Ewbank, Westmerland (Waller)	48b
EWRE, William, Lord	49d
Exeter (Salter)	40b
EYVES, Richard, of Bradley and Fishwick, Lancashire	42c

INDEX.

Fairbank, Cumberland (Musgrave)	39*a*
Fanshaw, Richard, of Barking, co. Essex	40*c*
FARR, John, of Epworth, Lincolnshire	45*a*
FARRAR, Sir Henry, of Skillingthorp, Lincolnshire.	30*c*
FAWCET, Samuel, of Broad-street, in the City of London	45*b*
Felton, Northumberland (Mallory)	50*b*
Fence, Lancashire (Thornton)	44*c*
FENWICK, John, of Crookden, co. Northumberland	46*a*
FENWICK, Robert, of Westmasin, co. Northumberland	46*a*
FENWICK, Thomas, of Brestwick, co. Northumberland	46*b*
FENWICK, Sir William, of Meldon, co. Northumberland, Knight	46*a*
FENWICK, Sir William, of Scrimarston, co. Durham	39*d*
FENWICK, William, of Blagden, co. Northumberland	46*b*
FERNES, Henry, of Walderswick, co. Suffolk	51*a*
Ferringsby, Yorkshire (Knavesborough)	50*a*
Feversham, Kent (Trout)	41*a*
FINES, Norris	51*a*
Fishwick, Lancashire (Sudel)	41*d*
——————— (Eyves)	42*c*
——————— (Kellet)	43*a*
Fittleford, Dorsetshire (White)	40*b*
FITZ-JAMES, Joan, Dorsetshire	22*d*
FITZ-JAMES, Leweson, Dorsetshire	22*d*
FIZAKERLEY, Nicholas, of Fizakerley, Lancashire	42*c*
FIZAKERLEY, Robert, of Walton, Lancashire	42*c*
Fizakerley, Lancashire (Fizakerley)	42*c*
——————— (Stannanaught)	44*a*
FLEETWOOD, Charles	21*a*; 36*b*
FLEETWOOD, Frances	21*a*; 36*b*
FLEMING, John, co. Cumberland	48*c*
FLEMING, William, of Riddal, co. Westmerland	48*b*
FLETCHER, John, of Burscoe, Lancashire	42*c*
FLINTOFT, William, of Scarborough, Yorkshire	48*c*
FLYER, William, of Llandilloportholi (Yeoman) Monmouthshire	45*c*
Fockerby, Yorkshire (Winsor)	49*b*
FORCER, John, of Haberhouse, co. Durham	30*a*
FORD, Robert, of Crewkhern, Somersetshire	46*d*
Fornby, Lancashire (Norris)	43*c*
FORSTER, Mr., of Brentford, co. Middlesex	45*b*
Foulforth, Yorkshire (Marshal)	49*a*
FOWEL, Henry, of Abbots-An, co. Southampton	47*b*
FOWL, Robert, of Billington, Lancashire	42*c*

FOWLER, Walter, of St. Thomas, Staffordshire	30*b*
FOX, Edward, of Rheteskin, Montgomeryshire	50*c*
Foxdenton, Lancashire (Ratcliff)	41*c*
FOXLEY, Thomas	29*b*
FRANCIS, John, at the Wardrobe, London	45*b*
FRANK, Marmaduke, of Kneeton	48*d*
FRANKLAND, William, of Woodhall, Yorkshire	48*d*
FREEMAN, Gabriel, of Thirsk, Yorkshire	48*d*
FREER, Robert, of Newbridge in Netherdale, Yorkshire	48*d*
FREWEN, Stephen, D.D., of the University of Oxford	38*a*
Frodingham, Yorkshire (Hunter)	48*d*
Frognal, Kent (Clark)	41*a*
Froom Vawchurch, Dorset	25*b*
FROSTER, Mr., of Brentwood, co. Middlesex	45*b*
Fryth-wood	27*c*
Fulwood, Lancashire (Sud)	44*b*
Furnes, Lancashire (Carter)	41*a*
———————— (Crosland)	44*b*
———————— (Park)	43*d*
———————— (Wilkinson)	45*a*
GAGE, William, of Bentley, co. Sussex	47*d*
GALE, Robert, of Akeham-grange, Yorkshire	50*a*
GALHAMPTON, Richard, of Newton-Ferris, Devonshire	39*b*
GAMUL, Francis, of Chester	38*b*
GARDNER, William, of Weymouth, Dorsetshire	40*a*
GARLAND, Augustine	5*d*
GARNET, Anthony, of Kendal, co. Westmerland	48*a*
Garston, Lancashire (Turner)	44*c*
GAY, Richard, of Lincomb, Somersetshire	46*d*
GAYLER, William, of Whitchurch (Yeoman), Dorsetshire	40*a*
GAYLERD, William, of Thorn, Somersetshire	46*d*
Gaynford, Durham (Sommerset)	39*d*
GELLIBRAND, Thomas, of Chorley, Lancashire	42*d*
GERRARD, Charles, of Halsal, Lancashire	41*b*
GERRARD, Sir William, of Ashton, Lancashire (Baronet)	42*d*
GIFFORD, John, of Eastbury, Berkshire	38*a*
GIFFORD, John, of Marston, Staffordshire	47*c*
GIFFORD, John, of Wolverhampton, Staffordshire	2*d*; 47*c*
GIFFORD, Peter, of Chillington, Staffordshire	30*b*
GIFFORD, Walter, of Hyon, Staffordshire	47*c*
GILES, Francis, Devonshire	51*b*

GILPIN, Christopher, of Kentmire, co. Westmerland . 48a
GODWIN, Richard, of Ilmister, Somersetshire (Yeoman) . 46d
Goldanger, Essex (Hills) 40c
Goldsmiths' Hall . . . 20d; 25a; 62b; 69b
GOODMAN, William, of Bramham, *alias* Bramwich, Yorkshire . 48d
GOODWIN, Robert 5c
GOOKING, Samuel 3d; 31b; 55d
Goosenargh, Lancashire (Midgeal) . . . 43b
——————————— (Parkinson) . . . 43d
——————————— (Trelfal) . . . 44c
Goosenargh cum Whittingham, Lancashire (Barns). . 41a
———————————————————— (Butler) . 42a
GORE, Edward, of Alker, Lancashire . . . 42c
GORSUCH, James, of Scarsbrick, Lancashire . . 42c
GOSLING, Anthony, of Moorsted, co. Southampton . . 47b
Gosworth, co. Chester (Hutchins) . . . 38b
Goul, Yorkshire (Empson) 49d
GOWEN, William, of Horsington, Somersetshire . . 46d
Gower, Anglicana, Glamorganshire . . . 27d
Gower, Wallicana, Glamorganshire . . . 27d
GRADEL, William, of Ulneswalton, Lancashire . . 42d
Grange, The, Kent (Philcot) 51a
GRANTHAM, Richard, of Halle, Chesbire (Yeoman) . . 38b
Graston-Leigh, Lancashire (Parkinson) . . . 43d
————————————— (Parker) . . . 44a
GRAY, Ralph, of Trumblehill, co. Durham (Yeoman) . 39c
Gray's Inn, Middlesex (Cook) 30a
Grazeley, Derbyshire (Turvile) . . . 39b
GREENHALGH, John, of Bramblesholm, Lancashire . . 41b
GREEN, Edward 68c
GREEN, James, of Tilsley cum Astley, Lancashire . . 42c
GREEN, Richard, of Bowerhouse, Lancashire . . 42d
GREEN, Richard, of Congleton, Cheshire . . . 38b
GREEN, William, of Lamoth, Yorkshire . . . 49d
GREEN, William, of Torisholm, Lancashire . . 41b
Greencroft, Durham (Hall) 39d
Greenlodge, Staffordshire (Dudley) . . . 47c
Greenwich, Kent (Coggan) 2b
Greenwich, East, Manor of . . . 4a; 22d; 31c
GRENVILE, Sir Richard, Knight, of Stowe, co. Cornwall . 1a
GREGSON, John, of Latham, Lancashire . . . 42c
GREY, Edward, of Chillingham, co. Northumberland . 2c

Grimlington, Yorkshire (Brockhouse)	48*b*
Grimlington, Yorkshire (Howden)	48*d*
Grimshaw, Nicholas, of Clayton, Lancashire	**42*d***
Grimshaw, Robert, of Clayton, Lancashire	**42*d***
Grimshaw, Thomas, of Clayton, Lancashire	**42*d***
Grimzargh, Lancashire (Houghton)	42*d*
Grisby, Yorkshire (Butler)	49*c*
Grismont, Castle of, Monmouthshire	26*a*
Guise, George, of Sandhurst, Gloucestershire	40*c*
Gunter, Bodenham, of Gwenthor, co. Brecon	50*c*
Gurdon, John	5*c*
Gwenthor, co Brecon (Gunter)	50*c*
Gwersey, Denbigh (Robinson)	2*c*
Haberhouse, **Durham** (Forcer).	30*a*
Haddockstone, **Yorkshire** (Berney)	49*c*
Haggerston, Thomas, of Haggerston, co. Northumberland	2*b*
Haggerston, Northumberland (Haggerston)	**2*b***
Hale, Cheshire (Hardye)	**38*c***
Hale, **Lancashire** (Norris)	**41*c***
Hall, William, **of Greencroft, co. Durham**	39*d*
Halle, Cheshire (Grantham)	38*b*
Hallifax, Yorkshire (Marsh)	49*a*
Hallows, Nathaniel.	25*a*
Halsal, Lancashire (Gerrard)	41*b*
Hamerton, Philip, of Purston, Yorkshire	50*a*
Hamilton, Duke of	2*d*
Hamilton, William	2*d*
Hampsal, Yorkshire (Washington)	49*b*
Harbert, Sir Edward, Knight, of Parsons' Green, co. Middlesex	1*b*
Harbert, Sir Piercy, Son of the Lord Powys	2*b*
Hardcastle, Edward, of Biggin, Yorkshire	48*d*
Hardwick, Thomas, of Shadwel, Yorkshire	48*d*
Hardwick, Monmouthshire (Jones)	45*c*
Hardwick, Manor of, Monmouthshire	27*b*
Hardye, William, of Hale, Cheshire	**38*b***
Harlaxden, Lincolnshire (Brailsford)	45*a*
Harnham, Northumberland (Winkle)	46*a*
Harper, John, of Dutton, Cheshire	38*b*
Harris, Christopher, of Chipping, Lancashire	42*d*
Harrison, Richard, of Overfrierside, co. Durham	39*c*
Harrison, Thomas, of Speak, Lancashire	42*d*

Harrowgate, Yorkshire (Hogg)	50*a*
Harup, Cheshire (Bostock)	38*b*
HARVEY, Edmund	5*d*
Haslewood, Yorkshire (Vavasor)	30*c*
Hassop, Derbyshire (Ayre)	2*d*
Hastings, Sussex (Rigate)	47*d*
HATTON, Peter, Cheshire	51*a*
HATTON, Sir Robert, of Bennyfield-Lawn, Kt., Northamptonshire	2*c*
HAUGHTON, Gilbert, of Brinseals, Lancashire	41*b*
HAUGHTON, John, of Parkhall, Lancashire	42*d*
Haughton, Lancashire (Berry)	42*a*
——————— (Lucas)	43*b*
HAWKINS, Peter, of Carperby, Yorkshire	50*a*
Hayton, Lancashire (Brockholes)	42*a*
Heaton, Lancashire (Brockholes)	51*b*
HEBDEN, John, of Clint, Yorkshire	50*a*
Helston, Cornwall (Collins)	38*a*
HEMSWORTH, George, of Roche, Yorkshire	48*d*
Henbury, in the Parish of Sturminster-Marshal, Dorsetshire.	40*b*
Henden, Manor of, Middlesex	23*a*
HERBERT, Lord	28*a*
HERBERT, Edward, Lord, of Ragland (Earl of Worcester)	26*c*
HERBERT, Henry, Lord	26*c*
HERBERT, Sir Percy, Knight	23*a*
Hern, Surrey (Wheeler)	47*d*
Herthead, Yorkshire (Amitage)	49*c*
HESKETH, William, of Northmeals, Lancashire	42*d*
Hesleside, Northumberland (Carlton)	46*a*
HIDE, Anthony, of Woodhouse, co. Southampton	47*b*
HIDE, Edward, of Purton, Wiltshire	1*c*
HILL, Robert, of Woodberry, Devonshire	39*b*
HIILS, John, of Goldanger, co. Essex	40*c*
HILTON, John, of Hilton, co. Durham	39*c*
Hilton, Durham (Hilton)	39*c*
HINDLEY, Lancashire (Langton)	43*b*
HITCHIN, Thomas, of Normanton, Yorkshire	48*d*
HODGES, John, Eastquantonhead, Somersetshire	46*d*
HODGES, Luke	5*c*
HODGKEY, Thomas, of Burwardsley, Husbandman, Cheshire	38*c*
HOGG, William, of Harrowgate, Yorkshire	50*a*
HOLDER, Thomas, of South Wheatley, Nottinghamshire	45*d*
Holderness, Yorkshire (Viscount Dunbar)	30*c*

Holland, Cornelius	5o
Hollingborn, Kent (Culpepper)	1a
Hollinghow, Westmerland (Philipson)	48a
Holm, *alias* Holden, Devonshire (Keyes)	39c
Holtby, Marmaduke, of Scakleton-grange, Yorkshire	50a
Hooker, Margaret	23a
Hooker, Nicholas, late Goldsmith and Citizen of London	23a
Hope, George, of Doddleston, Cheshire	38b
Hopkins, Thomas, of Tintenhull, Somersetshire	46d
Horton, Sir Ralph, K.B., of Wittham, Somersetshire	1b
Hornby, George, of Standish, Lancashire	41b
Horncastle, Lincolnshire (Brand)	45a
Horsey, John, of Compton-Dundon, Somersetshire	46d
Horsington, Somersetshire (Gowen)	46d
Houghton, William, of Grimzargh, Lancashire	42d
Houghton, Little, Northumberland (Rodham)	46a
Howard, Sir Charles, Knight, of Croglin, co. Cumberland	39a
Howard, Sir Charles, of Plenmeller, co. Northumberland	46b
Howard, Edward, junior, of Eccleston, Lancashire	42d
Howard of Estrick, Lord	25a
Howard, Sir Francis, Knight, of Naworth, co. Cumberland	2b
Howard, **Ralph, senior**, of Sutton, Lancashire	42d
Howden, **John, Yeoman**, of Grimlington, Yorkshire	48d
Howick	27o
Huddleston, Andrew, of Hutton-John, co. Cumberland	39b
Hugton, Lancashire (Lathom)	43a
Huncoat, Lancashire (Birtwisle)	42a
Hungate, Philip, of Saxton, Yorkshire	30b
Hunter, Richard, of Frodingham, Yorkshire	48d
Hurwoodale, Yorkshire (Chapman)	48c
Hutchins, William, of Gosworth, Cheshire	38b
Hutton-John, Cumberland (Huddleston)	39b
Hyon, Staffordshire (Gifford)	47c
Ilford, Essex (Clerk)	40c
Ilmister, Somersetshire (Godwin)	46d
Ilston, *alias* Lunnon, Glamorganshire	27d
Ince-Blundel, Lancashire (Mollineux)	43b
——————— (Blundel)	30a
Inkling-green, Lancashire (Bond)	41a
Isle Abbots, Somersetshire (Drake)	46d

JACK, Thomas, of St. Just, co. Cornwall	38*a*
JACKMAN, Joseph, of Covent Garden, co. Middlesex	45*b*
JACKSON, Christopher, of Bold, Lancashire	43*a*
JACKSON, George, of York	48*d*
JACKSON, John, Yeoman, of Shap, co. Westmerland	48*a*
JACOB, John, senior, of Tavistock, Devonshire	39*b*
JANYON, George, of Blackrod, Lancashire	43*a*
JEAN, Joseph, of Liscard, co. Cornwall	38*a*
JENKIN, David, senior, of Cowbridge, Glamorganshire	2*c*
Jersey, Isle of	6*d*
JERVIS, Thomas, Dorsetshire	40*b*
JERVIS, Thomas, of Bruton, Somersetshire	46*d*
JOHNSON, John, of Willoughby, Lincolnshire	45*b*
JONES, Evan, of Stockton, Herefordshire	40*d*
JONES, Hugh, of Bridgewater, Somersetshire	47*a*
JONES, John, of Dingastow, Monmouthshire	30*a*
JONES, Nathanael, of Bridgewater, Somersetshire	47*a*
JONES, Thomas, of Lantrissent, Monmouthshire	45*c*
JONES, William, of Hardwick, Monmouthshire	45*c*
JOYCE, George, of Portland, Dorsetshire	36*a*
KAINS, Alexander, of Raddipool, Dorsetshire	40*b*
KAINS, William, of Roddipole, Dorsetshire	2*b*
Kathorp, Yorkshire (Constable)	49*d*
Kefennern, Flint (Dutton)	50*d*
KELLET, Richard, of Fishwick, Lancashire	43*a*
Kendal, Westmerland (Garnet)	48*a*
Kendal, Manor of, Westmerland	26*b*
Kentmire, Westmerland (Gilpin)	48*a*
Ketton, Durham (Bulmer)	39*d*
KEY, John, of Walmersley, Lancashire	41*b*
KEYES, Richard, of Holm, *alias* Holden, Devonshire	39*c*
Kidderminster, Worcestershire (Chauncey)	48*a*
KIDDS, Christopher, of West-witton, Yorkshire	48*d*
KILLIGREW, Henry, of Lanrack, co. Cornwall	30*c*
KILLINGBECK, Mrs. ——, of Killinghall, Yorkshire	50*a*
Killinghall, Yorkshire (Killingbeck)	50*a*
Kilvey, Glamorganshire	27*d*
KINASTON, George, of Eastwick, Shropshire	46*c*
Kingsley, Cheshire (Ruter)	38*c*
Kingsthorp, Northamptonshire (Lane)	1*c*
——— ——— ——— ——— (Clark)	45*a*

KINGSTON, Charles, of Nanton-Beauchamp, Worcestershire . 48*a*
Kington, Somersetshire (Wear) . . . 47*b*
Kirby, Lancashire (Stannanaught) . . . 44*c*
Kirbyknowl, Yorkshire (Constable) . . . 49*d*
KIRKBY, Thomas, of Upper Rawcliff cum Turnaker, Lancashire 41*b*
Kirkland, Lancashire (White). . . . 44*d*
Kitle, *alias* Kythal, Glamorganshire . . . 27*d*
Kittermister, Worcestershire (Chauncey) . . 48*a*
KNAVESBOROUGH, John, of Ferringsby, Yorkshire . . 50*a*
Kneeton (Frank) 48*d*
KNIGHTS, William, of Brinton, Huntingdonshire . . 38*a*
Knightwick, Worcestershire (Clent) . . . 51*a*
Knoctorum cum Woodchurch, Cheshire (Chantrel). . 38*c*
KNOWLS, John, **of Par,** Lancashire . . . 43*a*
Knoyl, Wilts (Toop) 47*d*
Kythal, *alias* Kitle, **Glamorganshire** . . . 27*d*

LABURN, William, of Torrisholm, Lancashire . . 43*b*
LAMB, William, of Turnham, Lancashire . . 41*b*
Lambrick, Somerset (Noss) 47*a*
Lamoth, Yorkshire (Green) 50*a*
Lamsham, Monmouthshire 27*b*
Lamyet, Somersetshire (Davis) . . . 46*d*
Lanarth, Monmouthshire (Morgan) . . . 45*c*
LANCASTER, John, of Reynel, Lancashire . . . 43*a*
LANE, Richard, of Kingsthorp. . . . 1*c*
LANE, Richard, of Marychurch, Northamptonshire . . 39*b*
Laneham, Nottinghamshire (Tirwhit or Tyrwhitt) . . 45*d*
Lanercost, Cumberland (Dacre) . . . 51*b*
LANEY, Doctor ——, of Peterfield, co. Southampton . 47*b*
LANG, Thomas, of Plimpton, Devonshire . . . 39*b*
Langarran, Herefordshire (Scudamore) . . . 40*d*
LANGDALE, Sir Marmaduke, Knight, late of North Dalton,
    Yorkshire 1*a*; 2*a*
LANGDALE, Marmaduke 2*a*
LANGDON, Walter, of Cavan, co. Cornwall . . 38*a*
Langfield, Arthur, of Seacroft, Yorkshire . . 48*d*
Langham, Essex (Wenlock) 40*c*
LANGTON, Abraham, of Hindley, Lancashire . . 43*b*
LANGTREE, Thomas, of Langtree, Lancashire . . 43*b*
Langtree, Lancashire (Langtree) . . . 43*b*
Lanivels, Cornwall (Porter) 38*a*

INDEX. 91

Lanrack, Cornwall (Killigrew)	30c
Lantrissent, Monmouthshire (Lewis)	45c
Lanvihangel, Brecon (Wintour)	50c
Latham or Lathom, Lancashire (Wainwright)	41d
——————————— (Gregson)	42c
——————————— (Moss)	43b
——————————— (Rigmaden)	44a
——————————— (Speakman)	44b
LATHOM, Edward, of Allerton, Lancashire	43a
LATHOM, John, of Hugton, Lancashire	43a
LATHOM, Richard, of Allerton, Lancashire	43a
LATHOM, Richard, of Perbold, Lancashire	43b
LATHOM, William, of Allerton, Lancashire	43a
LAUDERDALE, John, Earl of	2d
LAWRENSON, John, of Hugton, Lancashire	43a
LAWSON, John, of St. Anthonies, co. Northumberland	30b
Laystuff, Suffolk (Allen)	47d
Layton, Lancashire (Beesly)	41a
————————— (Bamber)	42a
Leak, Yorkshire (Danby)	49d
Learchild, Northumberland (Clavering)	45d
LECHMERE, Nicholas	5c
Legrum, Lancashire (Dobson)	42c
Leigh, Lancashire (Urmston)	44d
LEIGHE, Urian, of Adlington, Cheshire	38c
LEMAN, William	5b
Lemonden, Northumberland (Wray)	46b
Levercust, Cumberland (Dacre)	51b
LEVISON, Thomas, of Wolverhampton, Staffordshire	1b
Leweson, Dorset	22d
LEWIS, John, of Lantrissent, Monmouthshire	45c
LEWIS, William, of Torkesteth, Lancashire	41b
LEWIS, Doctor William, of Llanwyvy, co. Merioneth	50d
LEWKENOR, Christopher, of the Middle Temple	2d
LEYLAND, Ellis, of Woston, Lancashire	41b
LEYLAND, Richard, of Abraham, Lancashire	41b
Libberston, Yorkshire (Coulson)	49d
Lidney, Gloucestershire (Winter)	1b
————————— (Charnock)	40c
Lincomb, Somersetshire (Gay)	46d
Lindhurst, Hampshire (Chamberlain)	47b
LINDSEY, Thomas, of Rickerby, co. Cumberland	39a

Lineaker, John, of Widnes, Lancashire	43a
Linkhorn, James, of Bowyet, Hampshire.	47b
Liscard, Cornwall (Jean)	38a
LISLE, Lord	5c
LISLE, William	3d; 31b; 55d
LISTER, Thomas	5b
Litham, Lancaster (Clifton)	30a
LITTLE-JOHN, John, of Tavistock, Devonshire	39b
Littlethorp, Yorkshire (Newton)	49a
LITTLETON, Sir Edward, Baronet, of Pillington, Staffordshire	47c
LITTLETON, Sir Edward, of Little Shelsey, Worcestershire	48a
Littletondrew (Wells)	47d
LIVESEY, George, of Sutton, Lancashire	43a
Llandillo-Grassenny, Monmouthshire (Norris)	45c
Llandilloportholi, Monmouthshire (Flyer)	45c
Llanliddon, Denbigh (Roberts)	50c
Llanvitherrin, Monmouthshire (Stubs)	45c
Llanwyvy, Merioneth (Lewis).	50d
LLOYD, ——, of the City of London	45a
LLOYD, Doctor Hugh, of St. Andrews, Glamorganshire	40d
LLOYD, Tristram, Flintshire	50d
LODDERDALE. See Lauderdale.	2d
London, City of (Roydon)	2a
——————— (Lloyd)	45a
——————— (Tailer)	49b
——————— (Wollaston)	65a
LONG, Lislebone	5b
LONG, Robert, of Westminster.	1c
LONGLEY, Richard, of Millington, Yorkshire	50a
Lostock-Gralam, Cheshire (Wright)	38c
Lougher, Glamorganshire	27d
LOUP, Thomas, of Henbury, in the Parish of Sturminster-Marshal, Dorsetshire	40b
LOVELADY, Henry, of Alker, Lancashire	43a
Loveley, Lancashire (Parker)	43d
Lowkellerbey, Yorkshire (Carre)	48c
LOWTHER, Richard, of Engleton, Yorkshire	50a
LUCAS, Richard, of Haughton, Lancashire	43b
Lucton, Herefordshire (Wigmore)	40d
Ludwel, Durham (Emerson)	39c
Lunnon, *alias* Ilston, Glamorganshire	27d

INDEX.   93

Madely, Shropshire (Brook)	30*b*
Madesley, Lancashire (Nelson)	43*c*
Magor, Monmouthshire	27*d*
Magor Regis, Manor of, Monmouthshire	27*c*
MAIDWEL, Laurence	23*d*
MALLET, James, of Portsmouth, co. Southampton	47*b*
MALLORY, John, of Felton, co. Northumberland	50*b*
MANNATON, Pierce, of Stoak-Cliveland, co. Cornwall	51*b*
MANWARING, Randal	18*b*; 69*d*
MANWARING, Robert	15*c*
MANWARING, William, of Windle, Lancashire	43*b*
Marberry, Cheshire (Weeksteed)	38*c*
Marlington, Yorkshire (Singleton)	50*c*
MARLOW, Sir John, Knight, of Newcastle-upon-Tyne	2*c*
Marrick, Yorkshire (Bulmer)	49*c*
MARSH, John, Doctor in Divinity, of Hallifax, Yorkshire	49*a*
MARSH, Roger, of Goosenargh, Lancashire	43*b*
MARSHAL, Henry, of Foulforth, Yorkshire	49*a*
Marston, Staffordshire (Gifford)	47*c*
Marthingeringes-Grange, Manor of, Monmouthshire	27*c*
Marthering Ringes, Manor of, Monmouthshire	27*c*
MARTIN, Henry	5*b*
MARTINGDAL, Philip, of Blackrod, Lancashire	41*c*
Mary-Church, Devonshire (Lane)	39*b*
MASHAM, Sir William, Baronet	5*d*
MASON, William, of Slowley, co. Norfolk	45*d*
MASSEY, Richard, of Rixam, Lancashire	30*a*
MASTERS, Edward, of Wilsborough, co. Kent	40*d*
Mathern	27*c*
Mawdesley, Lancashire (Waterforth)	44*d*
Mawley, Shropshire (Blount)	46*c*
Mayland, Durham (Millet)	39*d*
Maze, Surrey (Weston)	30*b*
Meldon, Northumberland (Fenwick)	46*a*
MELLING, John, of Ince-Blundel, Lancashire	43*b*
MELLING, William, of Chorley, Lancashire	41*c*
MENNES, Sir John, of Winlaton, Knight, co. Durham	39*d*
MERCER, Andrew, of Derby	43*b*
MERRY, John, of Bressencoat, Derbyshire	39*b*
METCALF, Michael, of Little Ottrington, Yorkshire	50*b*
METCALF, Thomas, of Ottrington, co. Northumberland	50*b*
Michaelhaies, Lancashire (Rishton)	44*a*

Middle-Rason, Lincolnshire (Constable) .	45*b*
MIDDLETON, Sir John, Yorkshire .	50*b*
MIDDLETON, John, Yorkshire .	50*a*
MIDDLETON, William, of Stockhal, Yorkshire .	30*c*
Middleton, Yorkshire (Doleman) .	49*d*
Middleton-George, Durham (Pudsey) .	39*d*
Middleton on Rowe, Durham (Ascough) .	39*d*
MIDGEAL, Edward, of Goosenargh, Lancashire .	43*b*
Mierscough, Lancashire (Butler) .	42*b*
———————————— (Pearson) .	44*a*
———————————— (Thistleton) .	44*c*
———————————— (Westby) .	44*d*
Milburn Port, Somersetshire (Walcot) .	47*a*
MILDMAY, Francis, of Ammersden, co. Oxon .	46*c*
MILDMAY, Sir Henry, Knight .	5*c*
Miles Court, Manor of, Monmouthshire .	27*c*
MILLET, Ralph, of Mayland, co. Durham.	39*d*
Millington, Yorkshire (Longley) .	50*a*
Milverton, Somersetshire (Chilcot) .	46*c*
Mims, North, Hertfordshire (Coningsby).	40*d*
Minehead, Somersetshire (Baker) .	46*c*
Minting, Lincolnshire (Monson) .	45*b*
Mitton, Little, Lancashire (Sherburn) .	44*b*
MOLLINEUX, Edmund, of Ince-Blundel, Lancashire .	43*b*
MOLLINEUX, John, of Ince-Blundel, Lancashire .	43*b*
Monmouth, Castle of, Monmouthshire .	26*a*
Monmouth, Manor of, Monmouthshire .	26*a*
MONSON, John, of Minting, Lincolnshire .	45*b*
MOOR, George, of Culhampton, Devonshire .	39*c*
MOOR, James, of Willeton, Somersetshire.	47*a*
MOOR, Marmaduke, of Ordsal, Nottinghamshire .	45*d*
MOOR, William, of Derby .	43*b*
Moors Court, Manor of, Monmouthshire .	27*c*
Moorsted, Hampshire (Gosling) .	47*b*
MORGAN, Anthony, of Casebuchan, Monmouthshire .	45*c*
MORGAN, Henry, of Stoak-Edy, Herefordshire .	40*d*
MORGAN, John, of Pentrebach, Monmouthshire .	45*c*
MORGAN, John, of Trawsby-mill, Merionethshire .	50*d*
MORGAN, John, formerly of Trostrey, now of Lanarth, Monmouthshire .	45*c*
MORGAN, William, of Wrengochin, Monmouthshire .	45*c*
MORLEY, Cuthbert .	23*d*

Morley, Cutbert, of Seymour, Yorkshire	3a
Morley and Mounteagle, Henry, Lord	40d
Morley, Sir John, of Newcastle-upon-Tine, Knight	39d
Morley, John, of Whorlton, Yorkshire	49a
Morley, Nicholas, of Standerber, Yorkshire	50b
Morley, Thomas, of Burton, Yorkshire	49a
Morley, Thomas, of Wymington, Lancashire	43c
Morley, Cheshire (Pool)	38c
Moss, Henry, of Skelmersdale, Lancashire	43c
Moss, Richard, of Lathom, Lancashire	43b
Moss, Richard, of Skelmersdale, Lancashire	43c
Mossock, Henry, of Bickerstaff, Lancashire	43c
Mounson, John, of Minting, Lincolnshire	45b
Mountague, Somersetshire (Chaffey)	46d
Mounteagle, Henry, Lord	40d
Mowbrick, Lancashire (Westly)	44d
Mowsey, Anthony, of Cattam, co. Suffolk	47d
Moyle, John	5c
Mumford, Edmund, of Weerham, co. Norfolk	45d
Musgrave, Sir Philip, of Cadwel, co. Cumberland	1a
Musgrave, Simon, of Fairbank, co. Cumberland	39a
Musgrave, Sir William, of Fairbank, Knight, co. Cumberland	39a
Mussel Hill, Middlesex (Benion)	2b
Myerscow, Lancaster (Tilsley)	1c
Naburn, Yorkshire (Palms)	50b
Nafferton, Northumberland (Swinborn)	46b
Nanton-Beauchamp, Worcestershire (Kingston)	48a
Nash, Dorsetshire (Coplestone)	40a
Nash, Hampshire (Chamberlain)	47b
Naworth, Cumberland (Howard)	2b
Nayler, Thomas, of the Bail, Lincolnshire	45b
Naylor, William, of Croston, Lancashire	43c
Neesam Abby, Yorkshire (Braithwait)	39d
Nelson, Henry, of Madesley, Lancashire	43c
Nelson, Thomas, of Wrightington, Lancashire	43c
Netherdale, Yorkshire (Freer)	48d
Nethersole, Francis, of Ash, co. Kent	40d
Netherstow, Somersetshire (Walker)	47a
Netherwitton, Northumberland (Thornton)	46b
Nevil, Edward	5c
Nevil, Henry	5c

NEWBERRY, Zachary, of Stockland, Dorsetshire	40*b*
Newbold, Leicestershire (Atterton)	45*a*
NEWCASTLE, Earl of	1*a*
Newcastle, Yorkshire (Redman)	49*a*
Newcastle-upon-Tyne (Marlow)	2*c*
——————————— (Riddle)	2*d*
——————————— (Morley)	39*d*
New-Church, Monmouthshire	27*b*; 27*c*
NEWCOURT, Richard, of Sumerton, Somersetshire	47*a*
NEWSHAM, Andrew, of Little-Plumpton, Lancashire	43*c*
NEWSHAM, Nicholas, of Little-Plumpton, Lancashire	43*c*
Newsham, Northumberland (Cramlington)	46*a*
Newsted Abby, Nottingham (Byron)	1*b*
Newtimber, Sussex (Bellingham)	47*d*
NEWTON, Miles, of Littlethorp, Yorkshire	49*a*
Newton Ferris, Devonshire (Galhampton)	39*b*
NICHOLAS, **Sir Edward,** of Westminster, Knight	2*a*
NICHOLSON, Christopher, of Tatham, Lancashire	41*c*
Nidd, Yorkshire (Trapps)	50*c*
Nillemondswich, Northumberland **(Ridley)**	46*a*
Nockton, Lincolnshire (Townley)	2*b*
Normanton, Yorkshire (Hitchin)	48*d*
NORRIS, Edward, of Hale, Lancashire	41*c*
NORRIS, Philip, of Fornby, Lancashire	43*c*
NORRIS, Walter, of Llandillo-Grassenny, Monmouthshire	45*c*
NORRIS, William, of Adlington, Lancashire	43*c*
NORRIS, William, of Blackrod, Lancashire	43*c*
NORTH, Charles, of Whitguift, Yorkshire	49*a*
NORTH, Richard, junior, of Docker, Lancashire	43*c*
Northmeals, Lancashire (Hesketh)	42*d*
NORTON, Doctor, of Colchester, co. Essex	40*c*
Noss, William, of Lambrick, Somersetshire	47*a*
NOUDIKE, George, of Wellam, Yorkshire	49*a*
Nunney, Somersetshire (Prater)	47*a*
NUT, James	5*d*
OGLE, Thomas, of Darrashal, co. Northumberland	46*a*
Okeham, Castle and Castle-yard of, Rutland	21*d*
Oldcleeve, Somersetshire (Pointz)	47*b*
Oldlaund, Lancashire (Robinson)	41*d*
Oldstcastle, Cheshire (Sharman)	38*c*
Olentight, Kent (Thornhil)	24*b*

Orchard, Devonshire (Wood)	39*c*
Ordsal, Nottinghamshire (Moor)	45*d*
ORTON, Francis, of Woodplumpton, **Lancashire**	43*d*
Osbulstone, Lancashire (Ward)	41*d*
Ottrington, Yorkshire (Metcalf)	50*b*
Ottrington, Little, Yorkshire (Metcalf)	50*b*
Outrawcliff, Lancashire (Butler)	42*a*
——————————— (Richardson)	41*c*
Overfrierside, Durham (Harrison)	39*c*
Oxford (Aston)	3*a*
——— (Chamberlain)	50*d*
Oxford, University of (Frewen)	38*a*
Oystermouth, Glamorganshire	27*d*
PAIN, Nicholas, of Causeway in Roddipol, Dorsetshire	40*b*
PALMS, Sir George, of Naburn, Yorkshire	50*b*
Pannington, Gloucestershire (Rolles)	40*c*
PAR, Ralph, of Altham, Lancashire	43*d*
Par, Lancashire (Knowls)	43*a*
PARK, Giles, of Furnes, Lancashire	43*d*
PARK, Lawrence, of Cuesdal, Lancashire	41*c*
PARKER, John, of Bradkirk, Lancashire	43*d*
PARKER, John, of Loveley, Lancashire	43*d*
PARKER, John, of Kendal, co. Westmerland	48*a*
PARKER, John, of Raddampark, Yorkshire	49*a*
PARKER, Thomas, of Graston-Leigh, Lancashire	44*a*
PARKER, William, of Woolfal, Lancashire	43*d*
Parkhall, Lancashire (Haughton)	42*d*
PARKINSON, Lawrence, of Goosenargh, Lancashire	43*d*
PARKINSON, Lawrence, of Swinshead, Lancashire	43*d*
PARKINSON, Thomas, of Clawton, Lancashire	43*d*
PARKINSON, Thomas, of Graston-Leigh, Lancashire	43*d*
PARRIS, John, of Pudding-norton, co. Norfolk	45*d*
PARSONS, George, of Beeston, Cheshire	38*c*
Parson's Green, in Parish of Fulham, Middlesex (Harbert)	1*b*
Pascal, Staffordshire (Astley)	45*a*
PATTISON, Robert, of Sowerby, co. Westmerland	48*b*
Paulharburn, Yorkshire (Ellis)	39*c*
PEARSON, Thomas, of Mierscough, Lancashire	44*a*
Pellenny, Manor of, Monmouthshire	26*a*
Pennard, Glamorganshire	27*d*
PEMBERTON, James, of Whiston, Lancashire	43*d*

Pemberton, Lancashire (Scot) .	41*d*
Penreth, Cumberland (Rain) .	39*a*
Penrose, Monmouthshire (Scudamore) .	45*d*
Pentherry, Monmouthshire .	27*b*
——————— Manor of, Monmouthshire .	27*b*
Pentrebach, Monmouthshire (Morgan) .	45*c*
Pentrewarn, Shropshire (Edwards) .	46*c*
Perbold, Lancashire (Lathom) .	43*b*
PERCY, Henry .	2*d*
PERCY, John, of Stubswalden, Yorkshire.	50*b*
PERKINSON, Thomas, of Chipping, Lancashire .	41*c*
Perlloyd, Monmouthshire .	26*a*
Peterfield, *or* Petersfield, Hampshire (Laney) .	47*b*
PHILCOT, Philip, of the Grange, co. Kent .	51*a*
PHILIPSON, John, of Hollinghow, co. Westmerland .	48*a*
PHILIPSON, **Miles,** of Throp, Hampshire .	47*c*
PHILIPSON, Miles, of Tisbury, Wiltshire .	47*d*
PIKE, Henry, **of St. Decumans, Somersetshire** .	47*a*
PIKE, William, **of St. Decumans, Somersetshire** .	47*a*
PILKINGTON, Hugh, of Coppul, **Lancashire** .	41*c*
Pillington, Staffordshire (Littleton) .	47*c*
PINCHIN, John, of Shalden, Hampshire .	47*b*
PITCHER, Thomas, at Whitsonset, co. **Norfolk** .	45*d*
Plenmeller, Northumberland (Howard) .	46*b*
PLESHINGTON, Robert, of Dimples, Lancashire .	43*d*
Plimpton, Devonshire (Lang) .	39*c*
PLUMPTON, Sir Edward, Yorkshire .	49*a*; 51*a*
PLUMPTON, John, **of** Uslet, Yorkshire .	49*a*
PLUMPTON, John, **of** Waterton, Lincolnshire .	45*b*
Plumpton, Little, Lancashire (Newsham) .	43*c*
POINTZ, Giles, of Oldcleeve, Somersetshire .	47*b*
POMFRET, Anthony, of Eshur, co. Surrey .	47*d*
Pomfret, Yorkshire (Awstwick) .	48*b*
Ponthaulgh, Lancashire (Rishton) .	44*a*
Pont-Island, Northumberland (Errington) .	30*a*
POOL, Thomas, of Morley, Cheshire .	38*c*
PORTER, Richard, **of** Lanivels, co. Cornwall .	38*a*
Portland, Dorset (Joyce) .	36*a*
PORTLOCK, John, of Cirencester, Gloucestershire .	40*c*; 51*b*
Portsmouth, Hampshire (Mallet) .	47*b*
Poston, Manor of, Herefordshire .	26*b*
Pounstock, Cornwall (Tremain) .	38*a*

POWEL, James	24a
POWER, William, of the City of Durham.	40a
POWIS, *or* POWYS, William, Lord	2b; 38a
PRAT, Millicent, of Cherryorton, Huntingtonshire.	40d
PRATER, George, of Nunney, Somersetshire	47a
PRESCOT, Edward, of Standish, Lancashire	41c
PRESTON, William, of Ellel, Lancashire.	43d
Preston, Lancashire (Shepheard)	44b
PRICE, Herbert, of the Town of Brecon.	50d
PRICHARD, Nathanael, of Abergavenny, Monmouthshire	45c
PRIDEAUX, Edward, Attorney General	5c
Puckington, Somersetshire (Dorchester).	46d
Pudding-norton, Norfolk (Parris)	45d
PUDSEY, Michael, of Middleton-George, co. Durham	39d
PUDSEY, Peter, of Sheriff Hutton, Yorkshire	2a
PUDSEY, Ralph, of Stapleton, co. Durham	30a
PULLEN, John, of Bishop-Mouncton, Yorkshire	49a
Purcasseck, Manor of, Monmouthshire.	26a
Purston, Yorkshire (Hamerton)	50a
Purton, Wilts (Hide)	1c
PURY, Thomas	5c
QUADRING, Sir William, of ——, Lincolnshire	51a
Quenneborough, Leicestershire (Smith).	30a
QUICK, Richard, of Woolton-magna, Lancashire	43d
Raddampark, Yorkshire (Parker)	49a
Raddipool, Dorsetshire (Kains)	40b
Ragland, Monmouthshire (Somerset)	2d; 45c
RAIN, William, of Penreth, co. Cumberland	39a
RAINBOROW, Margaret	24b
RAINBOROW, Thomas	24b
RAINBOROW, William	24b
RALEIGH, Carew	5c; 25c
RALEIGH, Sir Walter	25c
Randelholm, Cumberland (Whitfield)	39a
RATCLIFF, Sir Edward, Dilston, co. Northumberland	30b
RATCLIFF, Sir George, of Colton, Knight, Yorkshire	1b
RATCLIFF, William, of Foxdenton, Lancashire	41c
Rawcliff, Upper, cum Turnaker, Lancashire (Kirkby)	41b
READ, Ralph, of Chirton, co. Northumberland	46a
Reckinden, Essex (Wortham).	40c

Redhouse, Yorkshire (Slingsby)	2b
REDMAN, Sir John, of Newcastle, Yorkshire	49a
REDMAN, Sir John, of Writon, Knight, Lancashire	41d
Redwick, Monmouthshire	27d
———— Manor of, Monmouthshire	27c
Reynel, Lancashire (Lancaster)	43a
REYNOLDS, Robert, Solicitor-General	5c
Rheteskin, Montgomery (Fox)	50c
RICE, Edward, of Crosby-parva, Lancashire	43d
RICE, James, of Crosby-magna, Lancashire	43d
RICH, Thomas, of Worthel, Devonshire	39c
RICHARDS, Andrew, Somersetshire	50d
RICHARDSON, John, of Crosby-Ravenswich, co. Westmerland	48b
RICHARDSON, Thomas, of Outrawcliff, Lancashire	41c
Rickerby, Cumberland (Lindsey)	39a
Riddal, Westmerland (Fleming)	48b
RIDDLE, Sir Thomas, Knight, of Newcastle-upon-Tyne	2c
RIDDLE, Sir Thomas, junior, Knight, of Newcastle-upon-Tyne	2d
RIDER, John, of Scarcroft, Yorkshire	50b
RIDLEY, Musgrave, of Nillemondswich, co. Northumberland	46a
Ridley, Cheshire (Egerton)	38b
RIGATE, John, of Hastings, co. Sussex	47d
RIGBY, Anthony, of Tillington, co. Sussex	47d
RIGBY, James, of Coppul, Lancashire	41c
RIGBY, John, of Standish, Lancashire	44a
RIGMADEN, George, of Latham, Lancashire	44a
RINGROSE, Fairfax, of Amotherby, Yorkshire	49a
RISHTON, Edward, of Michaelhaies, Lancashire	44a
RISHTON, Ralph, senior, of Whiteash, Lancashire	44a
RISHTON, Ralph, junior, of Whiteash, Lancashire	44a
RISHTON, William, of Ponthaulgh, Lancashire	44a
Ritton, Northumberland (Widdrington)	46b
Rixam, Lancashire (Massey)	30a
Roche, Yorkshire (Hemsworth)	48d
ROBERTS, John, of Bridge-water, Somersetshire	47a
ROBERTS, Doctor William, of Llanliddon, co. Denbigh	50c
ROBINSON, George, of Bretherton, Lancashire	41c
ROBINSON, James, of York	50b
ROBINSON, John, of Brereton, Cheshire	38c
ROBINSON, John, of Gwersey, co. Denbigh	2c
ROBINSON, John, of Oldlaund, Lancashire	41d
ROBINSON, Luke	5c

Robinson, Margaret, Yorkshire	50b
Robinson, William 3d; 31b;	55d
Roddipole, Dorsetshire (Kains)	2b
Rodham, John, of Little Houghton, co. Northumberland	46a
Roel, Rutlandshire (Bodenham)	45a
Rolles, Anthony, of Pannington, Gloucestershire	40c
Rootchester, Northumberland (Rotherford)	46b
Roscoe, John, of Dalton in Furnes, Lancashire	44a
Rothbury, Northumberland (Thirlwal)	46b
Rotheras, Herefordshire (Bodenham)	2d
Rotherford, Thomas, of Rootchester, co. Northumberland	46b
Roundhay, Yorkshire (Tempest)	50c
Roydon, Marmaduke, Merchant, City of London	2a
Rudby, Yorkshire (Errington)	39d
Rufforth, Lancashire (Salvage)	41d
Ruter, John, of Kingsley, Cheshire	38c
Rutter, Michael, of Croston, Lancashire	44a
Saint Andrews, Glamorganshire (Lloyd)	40d
Saint Anthonies, Northumberland (Lawson)	30b
Saint Arvan's, Monmouthshire . . 27b;	27c
Saint Bees, Cumberland (Wibergh)	39a
Saint Decumans, Somersetshire (Pike)	47a
Saint Huton, or Sheriff Hutton	2a
Saint Just, Cornwall (Jack)	38a
Saint Kenfreth, Castle of, Monmouthshire	26a
Saint Kynmarks, Manor of, Monmouthshire	27b
Saint Thomas, Staffordshire (Fowler)	30b
Salkeld, Henry, of Winton, co. Westmerland	48b
Salkeld, Lancelot, of Skirmingham, co. Durham	40a
Salkeld, Little (West)	39a
Salming-grange, Lancashire (Clifton)	42b
Saloway, Richard	5b
Salter, Anthony, of the City of Exeter, Apothecary	40b
Salvage, Richard, of Rufforth, Lancashire	41d
Salwey, Humphrey	5b
Samlesbury, Lancashire (Sowerbuts)	44b
Samuel, Arthur 3d; 31b;	55d
Samwaies, John, late of Bradway, Dorsetshire	40b
Sandhurst, Gloucestershire (Guise)	40c
Sandisk, Yorkshire (Carre)	48c
Sawyer, Lawrence, of Yarum, Yorkshire	40a

Saxton, Yorkshire (Hungate) 30*b*
SAYER, Lawrence, of Worsal, Yorkshire . . . 50*b*
Scakleton Grange (Holtby) 50*a*
Scale, Lancashire (Bradshaw) 42*b*
Scarborough, Yorkshire (Boynton) . . . 1*b*
——————————— (Flintoft) . . . 48*c*
Scarcroft, Yorkshire (Rider) 50*b*
Scaresbrick, Lancashire (Gorsuch) . . . 42*c*
Scarming, Norfolk (Anguish) 45*d*
SCASEBROOK, Edward, of Scasebrook . . . 30*a*
Scasebrook, Lancashire (Scasebrook) . . . 30*a*
Scor, Ralph, of Pemberton, Lancashire . . . 41*d*
Scrimarston, Durham (Fenwick) . . . 39*d*
SCUDAMORE, James, of Langarran, Herefordshire . 40*d*
SCUDAMORE, James, of Penrose, Monmouthshire . 45*d*
SCUDAMORE, Rowland, of Treworgan, Herefordshire . 40*d*
Seacroft, Yorkshire (Langfield) . . . 48*d*
Sealey, Scaly, Henry . . . 3*d*; 31*b*; 55*d*
SEDGWICK, Gabriel 45*b*
Sellet, Lancashire (Bains) 42*b*
SENHOUSE, John, of Ecclestone, Lancashire . . 44*b*
SERJEANT, John, of Derby 44*a*
SERJEANT, Robert, of Alcliff, Lancashire . . 44*b*
Severn, River, Gloucestershire . . . 27*b*
SEY, William 5*c*
Seymour, Yorkshire (Morley) 3*a*
Shadwel, Yorkshire (Hardwick) . . . 48*d*
Shalden, Hampshire (Pinchin) 47*b*
Shap, Westmerland (Jackson) 48*a*
SHARMAN, William, of Oldstcastle, Cheshire . . 38*c*
Sheepley, Yorkshire (Ambrose) . . . 48*b*
SHEFFIELD, Sampson 3*d*; 31*b*
SHELDON, William, of Curringham, co. Essex . . 40*c*
Shelsey, Little, Worcestershire (Littleton) . . 48*a*
SHELTON, *alias* Sheldon, William, of Curringham, co. Essex . 40*c*
SHEPHEARD, Robert, of Cliff Park, co. Northampton . 40*d*
SHEPHEARD, Thomas, of Preston, Lancashire . . 44*b*
SHERBURN, Robert, of Little-Mitton, Lancashire . 44*b*
Sherburn, Yorkshire (Constable) . . . 48*c*
Sheriff Hutton, Yorkshire (Pudsey) . . . 2*a*
SHERRATTON, William, of Elwick, co. Durham . 40*a*
Shobden, Manor of, Herefordshire . . . 26*b*

SHUTTLEWORTH, Richard, of Bedd	44a
Silferton, Devonshire (Bear)	39b
SINGLETON, James, of Marlington, Yorkshire	50b
SINGLETON, Thomas, of Dendron in Furnes, Lancashire	44b
Sithney, Cornwall (Arundel)	51b
SKELTON, George, of Witherel-Abby [Wetherall Priory], co. Cumberland	39a
Skewsby, Yorkshire (Ascough)	49b
Skillingthorp, Lincolnshire (Farrar)	30c
Skilmersdale, Lancashire (Travers)	41d
———————————— (Moss)	43c
SKINNER, William	3d; 31b; 55d
Skippar, Yorkshire (Bland)	48b
Skirmingham, Durham (Salkeld)	40a
SLAUGHTER, Edward, of Bishopsfrome, Herefordshire	40d
SLINGSBY, Sir Henry, Baronet, of Redhouse, Yorkshire	2b
Slowley, Norfolk (Mason)	45d
Smeaton, Great, Yorkshire (Vincent)	49b
SMITH, ———	50d
SMITH, George, of Quenneborough, Leicestershire	30a
SMITH, Henry	5b
SMITH, John, of Awdfield, Yorkshire	49b
SMITH, John, of Conow, Lancashire	44b
SMITH, John, of Euxton, Lancashire	44b
SMITH, John, of Whitwal, co. Westmerland	48b
SMITH, Sir Owen, Knight	21a
SMITH, Parris	50d
SMITH, Thomas, of Egton, Yorkshire	50b
SNART, Henry, of Bretherton, Lancashire	41d
Soddington, Worcestershire (Blount)	48a
SOMASTER, John, of Stoakenham, Devonshire	39c
SOMERSET, Lord Charles, of Ragland, Monmouthshire	45c
SOMERSET, Sir Charles, co. Southampton	27a; 28d
SOMERSET, Sir John, co. Southampton	27a; 28d
SOMERSET, Sir John, of Ragland, Knight, Monmouthshire	2d
SOMMERSET, Sir John, of Gaynford, Knight, co. Durham	39d
Sound, in the Parish of Wrenbury, Cheshire (Barnet)	38b
SOWERBUTS, Thomas, of Samlesbury, Lancashire	44b
Sowerby, Westmerland (Pattison)	48b
Speak, Lancashire (Harrison)	42d
SPEAKMAN, William, of Latham, Lancashire	44b
Spettsberry, Dorsetshire (White)	40b

Spry, **William**, of Blisland, co. Cornwall	38*a*
Stainton, Great, Durham (Coatsworth)	39*d*
Stalbridge, Dorsetshire (Burleton)	40*a*
Stampard, James, of Warton, Lancashire	**41*d***
Standerber, Yorkshire **(Morley)**	50*b*
Standish, Edward, **of Wooson**, Lancashire	38*c*
Standish, George, of Derby	44*b*
Standish, Lawrence, of Standish, Lancashire	44*b*
Standish, Lancashire (Hornby)	41*b*
——————— (Prescot)	41*c*
——————— (Brown)	42*a*
——————— (Rigby)	44*a*
——————— (Standish)	44*b*
Standon, Staffordshire (Vize)	47*c*
Stanley, Peter, of Bickerstaff, Lancashire	44*b*
Stanley, Thomas, of Bishopton, Yorkshire	49*b*
Stannanaught, Henry, of Fizakerley, Lancashire	44*a*
Stannanaught, Lawrence, of Kirby, Lancashire	44*c*
Stapleton, Durham (Pudsey)	30*a*
Starting, Timothy, of Uttoxeter, Staffordshire	47*c*
Stella, **Durham (Tempest)**	2*c*
Stephenson, **William, of** Thornton, Yorkshire	50*c*
Stoak, Lincolnshire (Coney)	**45*a***
Stoak-Cliveland, Cornwall (Mannaton)	51*b*
Stoak-Edy, Herefordshire (Morgan)	40*d*
Stoak under Hambden, Somersetshire (Chaffey)	46*c*; 46*d*
Stoakenham, Devonshire (Somaster)	39*c*
Stockhal, Yorkshire (Middleton)	30*c*
Stockland, Dorsetshire (Newberry)	40*b*
Stockton, Herefordshire (Jones)	40*d*
Stone, Staffordshire (Collier)	47*c*
Storey, Robert, of Ednol, co. Cumberland	39*a*
Stowe, Cornwall (Greenvile)	1*a*
Stowel, Edward	2*a*
Stowel, Sir John, K.B., late of Cudderstone, Somersetshire	1*a*; 2*a*; 23*c*; 24*b*
Stowel, John	2*a*
Stragul, Manor of, Monmouthshire	27*b*
Street, Somersetshire (Weech)	47*a*
Struggle, Manor of, Monmouthshire	27*b*
Stubs, Thomas, of Llanvitherrin, Monmouthshire	45*c*
Stubswalden, Yorkshire (Percy)	50*b*

Subboscos, Glamorganshire	27d
SUDEL, Lawrence, of Fulwood, Lancashire	44b
SUDEL, Richard, of Fishwick, Lancashire	41d
Sumerton, Somersetshire (New-court)	47a
Supraboscos, Glamorganshire	27d
Sutton, **Lancashire** (Howard)	42d
——————————— (Livesey)	43a
——————————— (Wadmough)	44d
Swanscy, Glamorganshire	27d
SWINBORN, **William**, of Nafferton, co. **Northumberland**	46b
Swinshead, Lancashire (Parkinson)	43d
TAILER, **John**, of London	49b
TALBOT, **John**, Dinkley, **Lancashire**	44c
TANDY, Philip	68c
TANKARD, Thomas, of Butterset, Yorkshire.	50c
TATHAM, Edmund, of Burton, Yorkshire	49b
Tatham, Lancashire (Nicholson)	41c
Tatton, Cheshire (Whalley)	38c
Taunton, town of	23c
Tavistock, Devonshire (Jacob).	39b
TEMPEST, **Sir Richard**, Baronet, **of Stella, co. Durham**	2c
TEMPEST, **Stephen**, of Roundhay, Yorkshire	50c
Temple, **The Middle (Lewkenor)**	2d
THEAKSTON, Sir William, of ——	49b
THIMBLEBY, Charles, of Carlton, Yorkshire	50c
THIMBLEBY, **Sir John**, Lincolnshire	51a
THIRLWAL, George, of Rothbury, co. Northumberland	46b
Thirsk, Yorkshire (Freeman)	48d
THISTLETON, Andrew, of Mierscough, Lancashire	44c
THOMPSON, George	5d
THOMPSON, William, of Eccleston-magna, Lancashire	44c
Thorn, Somersetshire (Gaylerd)	46d
Thorncliff, co. Cheshire (Bretland)	38b
THORNHIL, Richard, of Olentight, co. **Kent**	24b
Thornley, Lancashire (Doughty)	41b
THORNTON, Sir Nicholas, of Netherwitton, co. Northumberland	46b
THORNTON, Richard, of Fence, Lancashire	44c
Thornton, Lancashire (Bootle).	42a
Thornton, Yorkshire (Adamson)	49c
——————————— (Stephenson)	50c
Thorp Brantington, Yorkshire (Daniel)	50a

Thorpennow, Cumberland (Walker)	39*a*
THROGMORTON, Sir Bainham, of Clowerwal, Gloucestershire	40*c*
Throp, Hampshire (Philipson)	47*c*
THYNNE, Henry, of Biddeston, Wiltshire	47*d*
TICKLE, John, of Alker, Lancashire	44*c*
TICKLE, John, of Derby	44*c*
Tillington, Sussex (Rigby)	47*d*
TILSLEY, Edward, of Ashley, Lancashire	44*d*
TILSLEY, Thomas, of Myerscow, Lancashire	1*c*
Tilsley cum Astley, Lancashire (Green)	42*c*
Tintenhull, Somersetshire (Hopkins)	46*d*
TIRER, John, Shropshire	50*d*
TIRWHITT, see Tyrwhitt	45*d*
Tisbury, Wilts (Philipson)	47*d*
TITCHBURN, Sir Richard, Knight and **Baronet, of** ——	50*d*
Titherington, Cheshire (Worth)	38*c*
TOOP, Francis, **of Knoyl**, co. Wilts	47*d*
TOOTLE, Hugh, of Whitkel, Lancashire	44*c*
TOOTLE, John, of Chorley, Lancashire	44*c*
Torisholm, Lancashire (Green)	41*b*
—————— (Laburn)	43*b*
Torkesteth, Lancashire (Lewis)	41*b*
TOWNLEY, Charles, of Nockton, Lincolnshire	2*b*
TOWNLEY, Christopher, of Curre, Lancashire	44*c*
Towthorp, Yorkshire (Ellis)	48*c*
—————— (Barton)	49*c*
TRAPPS, Robert, of Nidd, Yorkshire	50*c*
TRAVERS, Peter, of Skilmersdale, Lancashire	41*d*
Trawsby-mill, Merioneth (Morgan)	50*d*
TRELFAL, Cuthbert, of Goosenargh, Lancashire	44*c*
TRELFAL, Wil., of Warton, Lancashire	44*c*
Trellects-Grange, Manor of, Monmouthshire	26*a*
Treludda, Cornwall (Burlase)	38*a*
TREMAIN, Degory, of Pounstock, co. Cornwall	38*a*
TRENCHARD, John	5*c*
TRENNICK, Richard, of Ugborow, Devonshire	39*c*
Trewithrah, *alias* Triveday, Glamorganshire	27*d*
Treworgan, Herefordshire (Scudamore)	40*d*
Triveday, *alias* Trewithrah, Glamorganshire	27*d*
Trostrey, Monmouthshire (Morgan)	45*c*
TROUT, John, of Feversham, co. Kent	41*a*
Trumblehill, Durham (Gray)	39*c*

Tunstal, Lancashire (Turvor) .	44*c*
Tunstal, Yorkshire (Cholmley)	48*c*
TURNER, George, of Garston, Lancashire.	44*c*
Turnham, Lancashire (Lamb) .	41*c*
——————— (Dalton)	42*c*
TURNOR, John, of Woottonfitzpain, Dorsetshire	40*b*
Turrington, Norfolk (Winde) .	45*d*
TURVILE, Pool, of Grazeley, Derbyshire .	39*b*
TURVOR, John, of Tunstal, Lancashire .	44*o*
TUTLOCK, Edward, of Kirby, Lancashire .	44*o*
Twisleton, Yorkshire (Beesley)	48*c*
——————— (Bains) .	49*o*
Tydenham, Manor of, Gloucestershire .	27*a*
TYRWHITT, William, of Laneham, Nottinghamshire.	45*d*
Ugborow, Devonshire (Trennick)	39*c*
Ulneswalton, Lancashire (Gradel)	42*d*
UNSWORTH, Edward, of Windle, Lancashire	44*d*
UNWIN, John, of Ennington, Hampshire .	47*b*
Uprawcliff, Lancashire (Westby)	44*d*
URMSTON, Richard, of Leigh, Lancashire .	44*d*
Uslet, Yorkshire (Plumpton) .	49*a*
Uttoxeter, Staffordshire (**Starting**)	47*o*
VALENTINE, Matthias	55*d*
VAUGHAN, John, co. Radnor .	50*d*
VAVASOR, Sir Walter, of Haslewood, Yorkshire	30*b*
VAVASOUR, John, of Willatoft, Yorkshire.	50*o*
VINCENT, Richard, of Great-Smeaton, Yorkshire	49*b*
VIZE, Humphrey, of Standon, Staffordshire	47*o*
WADMOUGH, Richard, of Sutton, Lancashire	44*d*
WAINWRIGHT, John, of Latham, Lancashire	41*d*
WALCOT, John, of Milburn Port, Somersetshire	47*a*
Walderswick, Suffolk (Fernes)	51*a*
Walgrave, Nottinghamshire (Bawd)	45*d*
Walkampton, Devonshire (Arundel)	39*b*
WALKER, John, of Little Budworth, Cheshire	38*c*
WALKER, John, of Netherstow, Somersetshire	47*a*
WALKER, Lancellot, of Thorpennow, co. Cumberland	39*a*
WALLER, Thomas, of Ewbank, co. Westmerland	48*b*
Wallingford House, City of Westminster	25*a*

Walmersley, Lancashire (Key)	41*b*
Walton, Lancashire (Fizakerley)	42*c*
WARD, James, of Osbulstone, Lancashire	41*d*
WARDER, Baron	40*a*
Wardrobe, The, London (Francis)	45*b*
WARING, Robert, of Chorley, Lancashire	44*d*
WARMSTREE, Thomas, Worcestershire	48*a*
Warton, Lancashire (Stampard)	41*d*
———————— (Trelfal)	44*c*
WASHINGTON, Darcy, of Hampsal, Yorkshire	49*b*
WASHINGTON, James, Hampsal, Yorkshire	49*b*
WATERFORTH, Hugh, of Mawdesley, Lancashire	44*d*
WATERTON, Mrs., Yorkshire	50*b*
WATERTON, Thomas, of Carraw, co. Northumberland	46*b*
Waterton, Lincolnshire (Plumpton)	45*b*
Watton, Lancashire (Conwel)	42*b*
Wavertree, Lancashire (Darwen)	41*b*
WEAR, Humphrey, of Kingston, Somersetshire	47*b*
Weavers-Hall	68*d*
WEBB, Roger, co. Suffolk	50*d*
WEBB, Thomas, co. Suffolk	50*d*
WEBSTER, Hugh, of Eccleston, Lancashire	44*d*
WEECH, Richard, of Street, Somersetshire	47*a*
WEEKSTEED, Thomas, of Marberry, Cheshire	38*c*
Weerham, Norfolk (Mumford)	45*d*
Weetley, Lancashire (Barker)	41*a*
Wellam, Yorkshire (Noudike)	49*a*
WELLS, Edmund, of Littletondrew	47*d*
WELLS, Swithen, of Eastly, Hampshire	47*c*
WELLS, Thomas, of Horncastle, Lincolnshire	45*a*
WELSH, Thomas, of Awton, Lancashire	44*d*
WENLOCK, ——, of Langham, co. Essex	40*c*
WENTWORTH, Lord, Son of the Earl of Cleveland	2*a*
WEST, Lodowick, of Little Salkeld, Prebend of Carlisle	39*a*
WESTBY, Francis, of Mierscough, Lancashire	44*d*
WESTBY, George, of Uprawcliff, Lancashire	44*d*
WESTBY, John, of Mowbrick, Lancashire	44*d*
Westmasin, Northumberland (Fenwick)	46*a*
Westminster, City of	25*b*
———————— (Long)	1*c*
———————— (Nicholas)	2*a*
WESTON, John, of Maze, co. Surrey	30*b*

West-witton, Yorkshire (Kidds)	48*d*
Wetherall Priory, Cumberland (Skelton).	39*a*
WETHERBY, George, of Whiston, Lancashire	44*d*
Weymouth, Dorsetshire (Gardner)	40*a*
WHALLEY, Jeffry, of Tatton, Cheshire	38*c*
WHARTON, Anthony, of Eppleby, Yorkshire	49*b*
Wheatley, South, Nottinghamshire (Holder)	45*d*
WHEELER, Christopher, of Hern, co. Surrey	47*d*
Wheelton, Lancashire (Whittle)	44*d*
Whiston, Lancashire (Pemberton)	43*d*
———————— (Wetherby)	44*d*
Whitchurch, Dorsetshire (Gayler)	40*a*
WHITE, George, of Spettsberry, Dorsetshire	40*b*
WHITE, Robert, Kirkland, Lancashire	44*d*
WHITE, Thomas, of Fittleford, Dorsetshire	40*b*
Whiteash, Lancashire (Rishton)	44*a*
White-Castle, Castle of, Monmouthshire.	26*a*
White-chappel (Witherow)	51*a*
WHITFIELD, Robert, of Randelholm, co. Cumberland	39*a*
Whitguift, Yorkshire (North).	49*a*
Whitkel, Lancashire (Tootle).	44*c*
Whitsonset, Norfolk (Pitcher).	45*d*
WHITTLE, John, of Wheelton, Lancashire	44*d*
Whitwal, Westmerland (Smith)	48*b*
WHITWEL, Stephen, of Cropton, Yorkshire	49*b*
Whorlton, Yorkshire (Morley)	49*a*
WIBERGH, Thomas, of St. Bees, co. Cumberland	39*a*
WIDDRINGTON, Sir Edward, of Cartington, co. Northumberland	46*b*
WIDDRINGTON, Henry, of Bootland, co. Northumberland	46*c*
WIDDRINGTON, Henry, of Ritton, co. Northumberland	46*b*
WIDDRINGTON, Ralph, of Cowel, co. Northumberland	46*b*
WIDDRINGTON, Sir Thomas, Knight, Sergeant-at-Law	5*c*
WIDDRINGTON, Sir William, of Widdrington Castle, co. Northumberland	1*a*
Widdrington Castle, Northumberland (Widdrington)	1*a*
Widnes, Lancashire (Denton).	41*a*
——————— (Wood)	41*d*
——————— (Carter)	42*b*
——————— (Lineaker)	43*a*
WIGMORE, Robert, of Lucton, Herefordshire	40*d*
WILBRAHAM, William, of Woodhaye, Cheshire	38*c*
WILKINSON, John, of Furnes, Lancashire.	45*a*

Willatoft, Yorkshire (Vavasour)	50*c*
Willeton, Somersetshire (Moor)	47*a*
Willoughby, Lincolnshire (Johnson)	45*b*
WILLS, John, of Chisleborough, Somersetshire	47*a*
WILMOT, Henry, Lord	2*o*
Wilsborough, Kent (Masters)	40*d*
Wimbish, Essex (Wiseman)	30*c*
WINCHESTER, John, Marquis of	1*b*
WINDE, Sir Robert, of Turrington, co. Norfolk	45*d*
Windle, Lancashire (Manwaring)	43*b*
——————— (Unsworth)	44*d*
WINKLE, Thomas, of Harnham, co. Northumberland	46*a*
Winlaton, Durham (Mennes)	39*d*
WINSOR, Frederick, Major, of Clains, Worcestershire	48*a*
WINSOR, William, of Fockerby, Yorkshire	49*b*
WINTER, Sir John, Knight, of Lidney, Gloucestershire	1*b*
Winton, Westmerland (Salkeld)	48*b*
WINTOUR, John, of Lanvihangel, co. Brecon	50*c*
WISEMAN, John, of Wimbish, co. Essex	30*c*
Wisset, Manor of, Suffolk	21*a*
Witherel Abby, Cumberland (Skelton)	39*a*
WITHER, George	29*a*
WITHEROW, Richard, of White-chappel	51*a*
Wittham, Somerset (Hopton)	1*b*
Witton, Yorkshire (Brigham)	49*c*
WOLLASTON, Sir John, Knight and Alderman of the City of London	14*d*; 34*b*; 65*a*
Wollaston, Manor of, Gloucestershire	27*a*
Wolverhampton, Staffordshire (Levison)	1*b*
————————————— (Gifford)	2*d*; 47*c*
WOOD, Henry, of Widnes, Lancashire	41*d*
WOOD, Thomas, of Orchard, Devonshire	30*c*
Woodberry, Devonshire (Hill)	39*b*
WOODCOCK, Thomas, of Brindle, Lancashire	44*d*
Woodhall, Yorkshire (Frankland)	48*d*
Woodhaye, Cheshire (Wilbraham)	38*c*
Woodhouse, Hampshire (Hide)	47*b*
Woodplumpton, Lancashire (Orton)	43*d*
WOOLDRIDGE, Thomas, of Acton, Husbandman, Staffordshire	47*c*
Woolfal, Lancashire (Parker)	43*d*
Woolton-magna, Lancashire (Allenson)	41*a*
——————————— (Quick)	43*d*

Wooson, Lancashire (Standish) . . . 38*c*
Woottonfitzpain, Dorset (Turnor) . . . 40*b*
WORCESTER, Edward, Earl of . . . 1*b*; 26*c*; 28*d*
WORCESTER, Henry, Earl of . . . 27*a*; 28*d*
Worcester-house, in the Strand . . . 20*c*
Worsal, Yorkshire (Clifton) 49*d*
——————— (Sayer) 50*b*
WORTH, Peter, of Titherington, Cheshire. . . 38*c*
WORTHAM, Thomas, of Reckinden, co. Essex . . 40*c*
Worthel, Devonshire, (Rich) 39*c*
Woston, Lancashire (Leyland). . . . 41*b*
WRAY, George, of Lemonden, co. Northumberland . . 46*b*
WRAY, Thomas, of Beamish, co. Durham. . . 40*a*
Wrengochin, Monmouthshire (Morgan) . . . 45*c*
WRIGHT, Ellis, of Croston, Lancashire . . . 41*d*
WRIGHT, Peter, of Lostock-Gralam, Cheshire . . 38*c*
WRIGHT, Timothy, of the City of Westminster . . 45*b*
Wrightington, Lancashire (Nelson) . . . 43*c*
Writon, Lancashire (Redman). . . . 41*d*
Wye River, Gloucestershire 27*b*
Wymington, Lancashire (Morley) . . . 43*c*
Wysham, Manor of, Monmouthshire . . . 26*a*

Yarum, **Yorkshire** (Sawyer) 40*a*
Yealand, Lancashire (Chorley) . . . 42*b*
York (Bowes) 48*c*
—— (Jackson) 48*d*
—— (Robinson) 50*b*
YOUNG, Andrew (late called Sir Andrew Young, Knight), co.
   York 40*a*; 50*c*

ERRATUM.

P. 42*d*, *for* "William Houghton" *read* "William Haughton."

www.ingramcontent.com/pod-product-compliance
Lightning Source LLC
Chambersburg PA
CBHW021940160426
43195CB00011B/1171